CULTURES OF THE WORLD
Scotland

Cavendish
Square

New York

Published in 2020 by Cavendish Square Publishing, LLC
243 5th Avenue, Suite 136, New York, NY 10016
Copyright © 2020 by Cavendish Square Publishing, LLC

Third Edition

This publication represents the opinions and views of the author based on his or her personal experience, knowledge, and research. The information in this book serves as a general guide only. The author and publisher have used their best efforts in preparing this book and disclaim liability rising directly or indirectly from the use and application of this book.

All websites were available and accurate when this book was sent to press.

Cataloging-in-Publication Data

Names: Levy, Patricia. | Ong, Jacqueline. | Nevins, Debbie.
Title: Scotland / Patricia Levy, Jacqueline Ong, and Debbie Nevins.
Description: Third edition. | New York : Cavendish Square, 2020. | Series: Cultures of the world | Includes glossary and index.
Identifiers: ISBN 9781502650788 (library bound) | ISBN 9781502650795 (ebook)
Subjects: LCSH: Scotland--Juvenile literature.
Classification: LCC DA762.L48 2020 | DDC 941.1--dc23

Writers, Patricia Levy and Jacqueline Ong; Debbie Nevins, third edition
Editorial Director, third edition: Katherine Kawa
Editor, third edition: Debbie Nevins
Art Director, third edition: Andrea Davison-Bartolotta
Designer, third edition: Jessica Nevins
Production Manager, third edition: Rachel Rising
Picture Researcher, third edition: Jessica Nevins

PICTURE CREDITS

Printed in the United States of America

CONTENTS

SCOTLAND TODAY

Oh Flower of Scotland
When will we see
Your like again,
That fought and died for
Your wee bit Hill and Glen
And stood against him
Proud Edward's Army,
And sent him homeward
Tae think again.

SCOTLAND DOESN'T HAVE AN OFFICIAL NATIONAL ANTHEM, but if it did, those might be the opening lyrics. "Flower of Scotland" commemorates the Battle of Bannockburn in 1314 when Robert the Bruce, King of the Scots, defeated Edward II, King of England—and it serves as Scotland's de facto national anthem.

People enjoy a sunny June day in Kelvingrove Park in Glasgow. The main building of Glasgow University rises on the hill behind them.

Scotland is a country in the British Isles. It occupies the upper third of the island of Great Britain, while England and Wales take up the rest of the island. As a part of the United Kingdom (a union of England, Scotland, Wales, and Northern Ireland), Scotland's actual national anthem is "God Save the Queen"—the queen, of course, being Queen Elizabeth II of England. It is perhaps odd, then, that one of Scotland's most beloved informal anthems celebrates an ancient victory over England.

Today, Scotland's relationship with England is very good. The two countries share a great deal of history and culture, but Scotland is not merely a smaller, northern version of England. For centuries, it has maintained a separate and distinct identity and a vigorous sense of national pride, even as it has been overshadowed by its more powerful southern neighbor.

When people think of Scotland, they often think of tartan kilts, the haunting drone of bagpipes, mist-shrouded castles, and mythical creatures. These things

are not the stuff of ordinary daily life in today's Scotland, where jobs, schools, family, politics, and big questions like independence matter as much as they do anywhere. However, Scotland is a particularly fanciful place, filled with the magical stories of Celtic myths and legends. The country's national animal, after all, is the unicorn!

One mythical beast in particular never fails to fascinate. Just when it seems there's nothing left to say about the infamous Loch Ness Monster, "she" pops back into the news again. "Nessie," the mysterious creature that, according to folklore, inhabits the murky depths of Loch (Lake) Ness in the Scottish Highlands, first attracted modern attention in 1933. Sightings have continued ever since, though most have been discredited. Still, the idea that a prehistoric marine creature lives in Scotland's second-deepest lake simply won't die. Meanwhile, a healthy tourist industry has sprung up in the region, catering to seekers and believers.

The ruins of Urquhart Castle high above Loch Ness are a ghostly vision of the past.

This sculpture, called *The Kelpies*, celebrates the mythological and historical spirit of Scotland.

Like so much else in Scotland, the lore of Nessie goes back centuries to ancient times. The Irish monk Saint Columba, who brought Christianity to Scotland in 565 CE, reported seeing a man attacked by a huge "water beast" in the River Ness, which flows from the loch. Fast forward to 2019, and some scientists from New Zealand have come up with a new theory. The researchers, who were extracting DNA from water samples, suggest Nessie might be some sort of giant eel—not as exciting as a living plesiosaur, but yet another notion to be added to the long list of Loch Ness Monster speculations.

While most Scots probably scoff at the mention of Nessie, their love for mythological lore pervades their poetry, music, and art. It can be seen in the whimsy of Robert Burns's poems; in the names of favorite foods like cock-a-leekie, chappit tatties, clootie dumpling, and rumbledethumps; and in the magnificently quirky Edinburgh Festival Fringe—the biggest, craziest arts festival in the world.

On the Forth and Clyde Canal, two fantastical equine creatures rear up nearly 100 feet (30 m) high. Completed in 2013, the sculpture is called *The Kelpies*, a reference to the mythical shape-shifting water spirits once thought to inhabit the lochs and "fairy pools" of Scotland. Kelpies usually take the form of a horse, but each possesses the strength and endurance of ten horses. These stainless steel kelpies, then, are a fitting tribute to the horses that once pulled barges on the canal, as well as to the strength, perseverance, and imagination of the Scottish people.

Not long ago, in 2014, the Scottish people voted on whether to declare independence from the United Kingdom. The referendum upheld the status quo, with a small majority voting to remain united. However, the question didn't go away.

Just two years later, the entire UK held a referendum, this one on whether to, in effect, declare independence from the European Union (EU). The EU is an economic union of European nations for the purpose of being a more competitive trade enterprise in the global marketplace. In other words, when it comes to international economic dealings, bigger is better. Presumably, EU members reap financial benefits from belonging to the union. However, in some matters, it has been necessary to give up national interests and control for the benefit of the whole. Some UK residents were not happy about that. In the end, the British exit, or Brexit, vote prevailed, with most of England opting to leave the EU.

Scotland, however, was of a different mind. Said Nicola Sturgeon, the Scottish first minister, "Scotland's 62 percent vote to remain in the EU counted for nothing. Far from being an equal partner at Westminster [where the UK government is based], Scotland's voice is listened to only if it chimes with that of the UK majority; if it does not, we are outvoted and ignored."

And so the question of independence bubbled up again. In April 2019, Sturgeon proposed holding a second referendum before the end of the Scottish parliamentary session in May 2021. With the pro-independence Scottish National Party (SNP) in power, it might still take place, but there's no guarantee this time that the UK will be willing to go along with a "yes" vote, should it occur.

Scotland may be small, but it is not meek. As Sir Walter Scott famously asked in 1772, "Where is the coward that would not dare to fight for such a land as Scotland?" This feeling is echoed in another patriotic ballad, "Scotland the Brave." This song, like "Flower of Scotland," has been widely used as a national anthem.

Land of my high endeavor
Land of the shining river
Land of my heart forever
Scotland the brave!

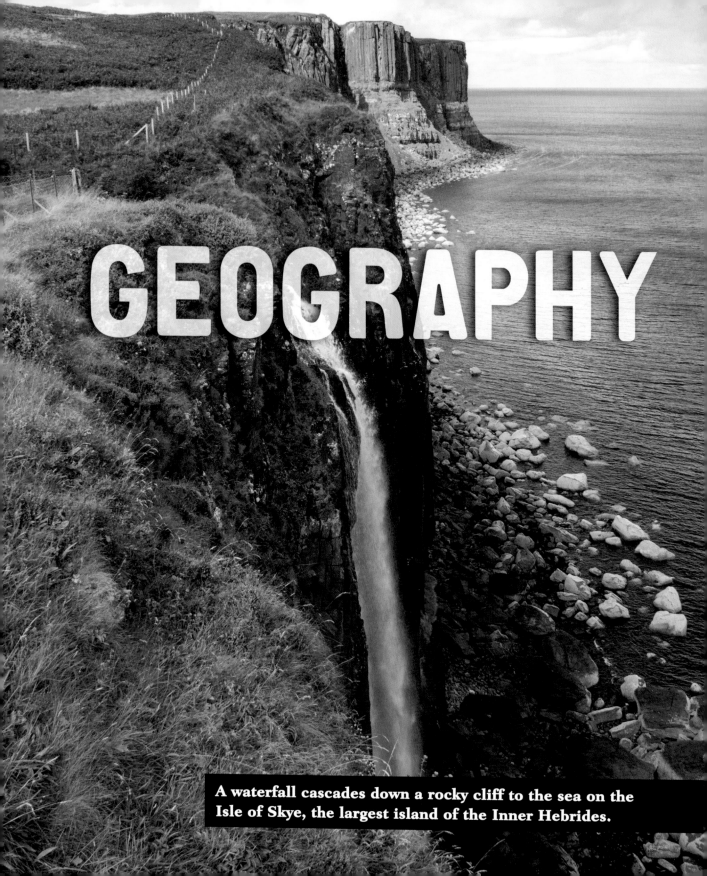

GEOGRAPHY

A waterfall cascades down a rocky cliff to the sea on the Isle of Skye, the largest island of the Inner Hebrides.

1

SCOTLAND IS A LAND OF RUGGED beauty. Its dramatically varied landscapes range from towering peaks to long, deep valleys, with mysterious lochs (lakes) and ancient castles, rocky shores and magical fairy pools, quaint fishing villages and bustling cities. The country is located on the upper third of the island of Great Britain. It is bordered by England to the south—its only land border—and is otherwise surrounded by water. To the west and north, it borders the Atlantic Ocean, and to the east, the North Sea.

Scotland's Shetland Islands are nearer to Oslo, the capital of Norway, than to London, the capital of the United Kingdom.

The mainland of Scotland consists of an area of 30,410 square miles (78,762 square kilometers), making it the seventeenth-largest country in the world. It has more than 790 islands (though only about 130 of them are inhabited), which have a total area of 2,149 square miles (5,566 sq km).

Scotland's mainland stretches 274 miles (441 km) from Cape Wrath in the north to the Mull of Galloway in the south, and 154 miles (248 km) from Applecross in the western Highlands to Buchan Ness in the eastern Grampians. Scotland's coastline is deeply indented by a series of fjords (or sea inlets), and very few places are more than 50 miles (80 km) from

Scotland comprises the northern third of the island of Great Britain, which it shares with England and Wales. Great Britain is not a country, but a geographical name for the largest of the British Isles. It's the largest island in Europe and the ninth-largest island in the world, in terms of area.

The name Great Britain (Britannia Major) came into use nearly a thousand years ago and was meant to distinguish the island from Britannia Minor, or Lesser Britain, which corresponded to the northwestern part of France, now called Brittany (or Bretagne in French).

The United Kingdom (UK), meanwhile, is a relatively recent political union of the countries of England, Scotland, Wales, and Northern Ireland. The nation takes up all of Great Britain and the northern one-sixth of the neighboring island of Ireland. Occasionally, the UK is referred to as Great Britain, but technically this is not correct.

UNITED KINGDOM

a coast. The distance between the Firth of Clyde and the Firth of Forth, which are the two great estuaries in the west and the east, is only 30 miles (48 km).

Scotland is a hilly country and can be divided into three geographic regions—the Highlands, the Central Lowlands (or Midland Valley), and the Southern Uplands. The Highlands make up two-thirds of northern Scotland. In Scotland, the mountains with peaks above 3,000 feet (914 meters) are known as Munros. They are named after the mountaineer Sir Hugh T. Munro, who in 1891 surveyed the country's mountains with peaks above 3,000 feet (914 m) and produced tables to catalog them. The tallest Munro is Ben Nevis, which stands at 4,406 feet (1,343 m) and is the highest point in Great Britain. The Great Glen, a geological fault line, divides the Highlands. Located in the Glen are a number of lochs (lakes), of which Loch Ness is the largest.

The Central Lowlands (or Midland Valley) is a part of Scotland that's home to the nation's main industrial belt. This triangular area includes Glasgow in the west and Dundee and Edinburgh in the east. Glasgow and Edinburgh are Scotland's two largest cities, and around 80 percent of Scotland's population lives in the cities and towns of the Central Lowlands.

The Southern Uplands is a hilly region, with elevations of up to 2,750 feet (838 m). There are also many fertile plains here. Scotland's highest village, Wanlockhead—located at 1,531 feet (467 m) above sea level—is in the beautiful area of the Southern Uplands known as the Lowther Hills.

ISLANDS

Scotland has more than 790 islands, most of which are part of the Hebrides to the west and the Orkney and Shetland island groups to the north. Of the 790 islands, only about 130 are inhabited, and just 62 exceed 3 square miles (7.8 sq km) in area.

THE HEBRIDES ISLANDS   This large archipelago lies off of Scotland's west coast. It's made up of two main groups, the Inner Hebrides, 36 inhabited islands that lie closer to the mainland, and the Outer Hebrides, a chain of more than 100 islands that lie farther out at sea. Only 15 of the Outer Hebrides are inhabited.

The Inner and Outer Hebrides are separated in the north by a strait called the Minch, and in the south by the Sea of the Hebrides. The main islands of the Inner Hebrides include Skye, the largest and northernmost of the main islands, Islay (EYE-la), Jura, Mull, Raasay, and Staffa. The main islands of the Outer Hebrides include Lewis and Harris, which is one island with two parts and which is also the largest and most northerly island of the Outer Hebrides; as well as Barra, Benbecula, Berneray, North Uist, South Uist, and the UNESCO World Heritage cultural and natural site Saint Kilda.

THE ORKNEY ISLANDS   Lying off the northeastern tip of the Scottish mainland, the Orkney Islands (also known as simply Orkney) are one of the two island groups called the Northern Isles. The other group is the Shetlands.

WORLD HERITAGE SITES

Since 1975, the United Nations Educational, Scientific and Cultural Organization (UNESCO) has maintained a list of international landmarks or regions considered to be of "outstanding value" to the people of the world. Such sites embody the common natural and cultural heritage of humanity, and therefore deserve particular protection. The organization works with the host country to establish plans for managing and conserving their sites. UNESCO also reports on sites that are in imminent or potential danger of destruction and can offer emergency funds to try to save the property.

The organization is continually assessing new sites for inclusion on the World Heritage list. In order to be selected, a site must be of "outstanding universal value" and meet at least one of ten criteria. These required elements include cultural value—that is, artistic, religious, or historical significance—and natural value, including exceptional beauty, unusual natural phenomena, and scientific importance.

As of January 2019, there were 1,092 sites listed, including 845 cultural, 209 natural, and 38 mixed (cultural and natural) properties in 167 nations. Of those, 54 were listed as "in danger." Out of the 29 sites listed in the United Kingdom, 5 cultural sites and 1 mixed site are located in Scotland: the Old and New Towns of Edinburgh, the Forth Bridge, New Lanark, the Antonine Wall (one of three sections that make up the listing "Frontiers of the Roman Empire"), the Heart of Neolithic Orkney, and the island of Saint Kilda (a site of both cultural and historical importance). Ancient structures on Saint Kilda are shown above.

Some 22,000 Orcadians live in Orkney. The largest of the seventy islands is Mainland, with an area of 202 square miles (523 sq km). Curiously, it's often referred to as "the Mainland," even though, geographically, it isn't actually the Scottish mainland at all. Meanwhile, the mainland itself is usually referred to as "Scotland." Orkney contains some of the oldest and best-preserved Neolithic sites in Europe, which has earned it a UNESCO World Heritage designation as the "Heart of Neolithic Orkney."

THE SHETLAND ISLANDS Also called Shetland, this other group in the Northern Isles of Scotland is a subarctic archipelago made up of about 100 islands. Shetland is home to about 23,200 rugged Shetlanders, and its capital, Lerwick, has a population of about 7,000. As in Orkney, the largest island is called Mainland. With an area of 373 square miles (967 sq km), Mainland is the third-largest of Scotland's islands and the fifth-largest of the British Isles. Shetland also includes another fifteen inhabited islands. The island group lies about 50 miles (80 km) northeast of Orkney. About 170 miles (280 km) to the northwest of Shetland are the even more isolated Faroe Islands, which are part of Denmark.

The remote location of the islands has led to the development of distinct animal breeds: heavy-coated Shetland ponies and long-haired Shetland sheepdogs, also known as Sheltie collies. There are also Shetland sheep, cattle, geese, and ducks—all hardy breeds.

RIVERS

There are twenty-six rivers flowing directly into the sea. The most important are the Forth and Tay, which flow from the Highlands, and the Clyde and Tweed, which originate in the Southern Uplands. The Forth, Tay, and Clyde open into large estuaries and support the major cities of Edinburgh, Dundee, and Glasgow, respectively.

CLIMATE

Scotland has a varied climate, but it is rarely extreme. Its geographic position in northern Europe gives it a temperate climate. The moderating influence of the Gulf Stream along the western coastline leads to fairly warm temperatures in some areas, even in winter. At the same time, because the Highlands, especially the Cairngorm Plateau, are the highest elevations in Britain, this area rarely loses its snow cover, even in summer. The Highlands often experience strong

"In Scotland, when people congregate, they tend to argue and discuss and reason; in Orkney, they tell stories."
–George Mackay Brown (1921-1996), Orkney poet

The rugged, rocky coasts of Scotland are riddled with unusual natural formations that rise out of the sea. These vertical columns of rock are formed by wave erosion of the headland and often take on dramatic shapes. Scotland has many such stacks, and they make for stunning landscapes, as well as homes and resting places for seabirds and other marine life. Many have fantastical shapes and fanciful names, in typical Scottish fasion.

Stac an Armin, which rises 627 feet (191 m) out of the North Atlantic Ocean, is the highest sea stack in the UK. Situated west of the island of Boreray, the massive rock is part of the Saint Kilda archipelago. The 449-foot- (137 m) high Old Man of Hoy, above, is another famous stack off Hoy Island in Orkney. Each year, about twenty daredevil climbers will ascend to the top of the Old Man, just for the fun of it. The pointed Stacks of Duncansby, rising almost 200 feet (60 m) at the northernmost tip of Great Britain, resemble giant witches' hats or arrowheads, depending on the view.

winds and cloud cover as well. Ben Nevis, for example, is exposed to gales that come from a southerly direction and can reach speeds of 120 miles (193 km) per hour for as much as two-thirds of the year.

In the northernmost areas, there is a significant difference between the lengths of the longest and shortest days. For much of summer, daytime can last for as long as twenty hours. The east coast has the most hours of sunshine and is less affected by the prevailing westerly winds. In the spring and winter, dry easterly winds often bring cold continental air masses to the country. Rainfall is variable, with the Highlands receiving more than 118 inches (300 centimeters) of rain a year, whereas the east coast gets as little as 25 inches (64 cm) of rain in some years.

FLORA

During the past century, human activity has put a large number of plant species in Britain on the verge of extinction. Nonetheless, many rare plants can still be found in Scotland. The mild climate of the southwest supports delicate plants, whereas the Highlands are home to plants more commonly seen in the Arctic.

One endangered habitat still found in the Scottish mountains is the raised bog. Raised bogs are peatland ecosystems that develop in lowland areas such as topographic depressions, the heads of estuaries,

An insect stuck on the sticky leaves of a *Drosera anglica* will become the carnivorous great sundew plant's next meal.

and river floodplains. Raised bogs are largely dependent on rainfall for their supply of water and are formed by the decaying remains of mosses such as *Sphagnum balticum*. They are found on low plains or broad valley floors, and they support a distinctive community of plants (including the great sundew, Britain's largest carnivorous plant) and birds (such as the golden plover).

About 18.5 percent of Scotland is wooded. This is an improvement over the mere 5 percent of woodland that covered the country in 1900. Although it is home to both deciduous and coniferous trees, conifers are the most common, and they are cultivated as a cash crop. These quick-growing trees are deliberately planted close together so that they grow tall rather than wide.

At ground level, rare plants such as wintergreen (used to make medicine), twinflower (a tiny pink flower with two flower heads), and wood anemones can be found. Many of these rare plants are featured in Scottish songs. The national emblem of Scotland is the thistle, a prickly plant with purple flowers.

FAUNA

Scotland is home to more than ninety thousand species of plants and animals, some thirty of which are not found anywhere else. These include the Scottish crossbill, a crimson-colored finch; and the Scottish primrose, a small purple flower.

A wild stag stands majestically in the Scottish Highlands.

In the twelfth century, reindeer roamed freely in the valleys of Scotland. They were, however, later hunted to extinction. Recently, herds of reindeer have been reintroduced on the slopes of the Cairngorms. Also living in the mountains are red deer, a Scottish icon. The largest land mammal in Britain, the red deer stag (male) has distinctive antlers that it sheds at the end of winter. Around 250,000 red deer still survive despite culling, hunting, and the harsh winters.

The most magnificent bird to be found in the Scottish mountains is the once-endangered golden eagle. It now breeds happily in the Highlands. Named after its golden nape feathers, the golden eagle has a wingspan of around 7 feet (2 m) and hunts young sheep and other small mammals.

Scotland's natural woodlands are home to many unusual creatures such as the black grouse and the capercaillie, large game birds that used to be hunted. Another inhabitant of the woodlands is the Scots crossbill, whose only habitat is the Scottish pine forests.

Scotland has a long coastline of around 7,456 miles (12,000 km) and numerous offshore islands, which are resting places for migrant birds from the Arctic. These islands, many of them no bigger than a rock, also support colonies of Manx shearwaters, great skuas (one-third of the entire Northern Hemisphere's population), and hundreds of thousands of common seabirds. Scotland has 36 percent of the world's population of Atlantic seals, or gray seals, breeding around its shores, but in recent years they have been threatened by the increase in fish farms. Many are either poisoned by the chemicals used to prevent fish diseases or shot by fish farmers wishing to protect their stock.

CITIES

The four major cities in Scotland are Edinburgh, Glasgow, Aberdeen, and Dundee. All are located on the banks of Scotland's main rivers or estuaries.

EDINBURGH is the capital and is Scotland's second most populous city. About 518,500 people live in the city, which is perched on a series of extinct volcanoes in east-central Scotland between the Pentland Hills and the southern shores of the Firth of Forth. In the nineteenth century, Edinburgh was known for biscuits, breweries, and books. Today, however, its economy is driven largely by the services sector, particularly the areas of finance, science, and technology. Edinburgh serves as the headquarters of most of the Scottish banks and is an important financial center.

Edinburgh's other major industry is tourism. It is a modern, dynamic city where festivals, such as the Edinburgh International Festival, attract the world's leading performers and thousands of visitors, especially in summer. As Robert Louis Stevenson once wrote, "Edinburgh is what Paris ought to be."

Edinburgh continues to be the top destination for overseas and UK visitors to Scotland. The city is also Scotland's political center. The new Parliament Building was completed in 2004.

"Edinburgh is a city of shifting light, of changing skies, of sudden vistas. A city so beautiful it breaks the heart again and again."
–Alexander McCall Smith, author of the *No. 1 Ladies' Detective Agency* series and other novels

The clock on the famous Balmoral Hotel clock tower in Old Town Edinburgh is always three minutes fast—and has been since 1902.

The River Clyde flows through Glasgow.

GLASGOW has a population of about 626,410, making it Scotland's largest and most densely populated city, and it is the third most populous city in the UK. Residents of the city are referred to formally as "Glaswegians" or more casually as "Weegies."

The city is located along both banks of the River Clyde, 20 miles (32 km) from the mouth of the river, occupying most of the surrounding valley.

Glasgow is the commercial capital of Scotland, and it is the largest retail center in the UK after London. It is one of Europe's top twenty financial centers and is home to many of Scotland's leading businesses.

Glasgow was once notorious for its slum areas, especially an area called the Gorbals. It was also seen as an industrial center, but in the late 1950s, the city began a rebuilding program that saw many small companies move into industrial parks, decreasing congestion in the inner city.

Today, Glasgow is full of first-class sports and leisure facilities, internationally acclaimed museums and galleries, and stunning architecture, and it has a vibrant nightlife scene. Glasgow hosted the 2014 Commonwealth Games and the first European Championships in 2018. It also boasts a university that is five centuries old.

ABERDEEN is a thriving, cosmopolitan port in the northeast of Scotland. Situated between the Don and Dee Rivers, it is Scotland's third-largest city, with a population of about 227,560. In the mid-eighteenth to mid-twentieth centuries, it was known as the Granite City because its buildings incorporated locally quarried gray granite. Since the discovery of offshore oil reserves in the North Sea in the 1970s, however, Aberdeen has become the center of the North Sea energy industry and has been dubbed "the oil capital of Europe." Aberdeen is also home to the busiest commercial heliport in the world.

The city has two universities, the University of Aberdeen, founded in 1495, and Robert Gordon University.

DUNDEE is Scotland's fourth-largest city. Situated on the east coast of Scotland on the River Tay, it has a population of almost 150,000. Dundee has a long and rich history dating back to the Iron Age. By the fourteenth century, it was one of Scotland's most important towns. It was the main site of numerous battles, mostly between the Brits and the Scots. Like Aberdeen, Dundee has been influenced by the development of the North Sea oil economy. Other industries include shipbuilding and the manufacturing of jute, textiles, paper, sweets, and electronic appliances. It has recently become well known as a center for computer game creation and comic book graphic design.

The Tay Bridge extends over the river of the same name in Dundee.

Today, Dundee is sometimes called the City of Discovery because of the large number of scientific facilities found there. In 2014, UNESCO named Dundee as one of its first Cities of Design as part of its Creative Cities Network. The city also houses the Scottish Dance Theater and two universities.

INTERNET LINKS

https://www.nature.scot
The Scottish Natural Heritage website focuses on many nature-related topics.

https://scottishwildlifetrust.org.uk
The Scottish Wildlife Trust site provides information and photos about the country's plants and animals.

https://whc.unesco.org/en/list/387
The World Heritage listing for Saint Kilda is on the UNESCO site.

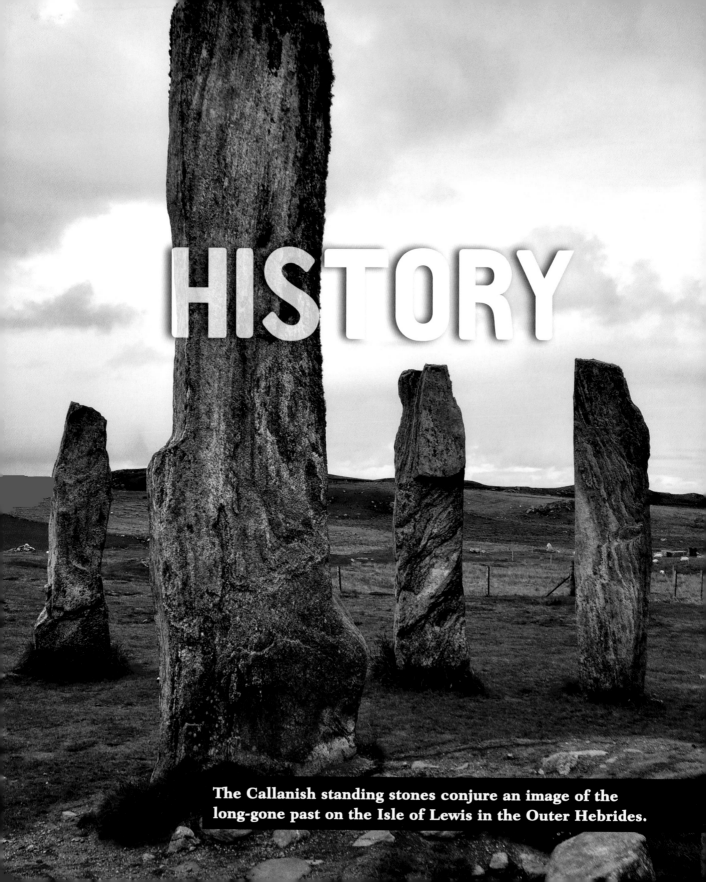

HISTORY

The Callanish standing stones conjure an image of the long-gone past on the Isle of Lewis in the Outer Hebrides.

2

SCOTLAND'S HISTORY GOES FAR back into the hazy mists of time. Written history begins with the coming of the Romans in 79 or 80 CE, but human history in this region extends back by thousands of years.

The first evidence of human habitation in Scotland dates from the Paleolithic era. An archaeological site at Howburn Farm near Biggar in South Lanarkshire, Scotland, dates to between 12,000 and 10,800 BCE. This discovery in 2005 changed historians' view of human habitation in Scotland, pushing it much earlier than had previously been known.

These early inhabitants from present-day England, Ireland, and northern Europe were hunter-gatherers and fishermen. Around the second millennium BCE, the inhabitants started to farm and raise livestock.

As the Neolithic farmers took on a sedentary lifestyle, they were able to build larger and more permanent dwellings and structures. These early inhabitants built megaliths, or stone constructions, that remain today. The Orkney Islands are a particularly rich site for Neolithic ruins, such as the chamber tomb at Maeshowe and the sophisticated stone houses at Skara Brae. The civilizations that built these grand tombs, houses, and standing stone monuments lived on the western and northern islands of Scotland. Although these places are now agriculturally barren (being largely peat bog), the land was much more fertile during Neolithic times, when the climate in northern Scotland was milder and drier.

Between 2000 and 1500 BCE, a Bronze Age culture was introduced to Scotland by the Beaker people from mainland Europe—so named by archaeologists for the shape of their drinking vessels. These people understood the process of bronze making and created metal weapons and tools for land clearance and farming. Remains of Bronze Age Scotland can be found at Callanish on the Isle of Lewis and Brodgar in the Orkney Islands.

The Iron Age developed in Scotland around 500 BCE through the Celts from Europe. They brought with them iron tools. Many of them lived in ring forts, banked earthen compounds with mud and wattle houses and often an underground passage for escape or storage.

ROMANS, VIKINGS, AND CELTS

When the Romans ventured to Scotland around 80 CE, they discovered a country with a number of Celtic tribes who grew oats and barley and hunted deer and salmon. Since they had tattoos, the Romans named some of these tribes Picts, which comes from the Latin *pictura*, meaning "painted."

Gnaeus Julius Agricola, the Roman governor of Britain, led the invasion of Scotland. He drove the Picts into the Highlands and built a series of stone forts on the land between the Firth of Forth (mouth of the River Forth) and the Firth of Clyde (mouth of the River Clyde), which is the narrowest point between the eastern and western shores.

It was not until the second century that a more permanent defense force was established along Hadrian's Wall. Named after the Roman emperor Hadrian, the wall was designed to keep the Celtic tribes out of England, an easier task than subduing them. A second wall was built twenty years later by Emperor Antoninus Pius, but it was rapidly abandoned. Today, most of the wall is gone, but some remains are visible, and they are part of a UNESCO World Heritage site called Frontiers of the Roman Empire. During the Romans' three-hundred-year stay in Scotland, some fifty thousand soldiers died guarding the border.

The Romans withdrew from Britain at the turn of the fifth century, leaving Scotland occupied by distinct ethnic groups. Successfully resisting the invasion of the Romans, the Picts staked their claim on the northern islands of Scotland and the north and east of the mainland. In the southwest were the Romanized Britons, who spoke a language ancestral to modern Welsh. The name Scot originally referred to the people who spoke Gaelic in Ireland and the west of

Scotland. Angles, who were Europeans from Bamberg in Germany, conquered an area in the southeast of Scotland in the sixth century.

At the end of the eighth century, another group influenced Scottish life—the Norse. They were a group of North Germanic people who inhabited Scandinavia between 800 and 1300 CE and spoke what is now called the Old Norse language. Commonly known as Vikings, they invaded all of the northern islands and then the northeast of mainland Scotland. The Shetland and Orkney Islands became the base for a Norse culture that spread to England and Ireland.

For several centuries, Pictish, Briton, and Gaelic dynasties intermarried and vied for supremacy in Scotland. The Gaels—another name for the Scots—were able to marry into the dynasties of the other Celtic peoples and assimilate them. Scots king Malcolm II came to power in 1005 after defeating and killing his cousin Kenneth III. Malcolm wanted to secure his family's right to the throne, and he wanted to expand the territory of his kingdom. He set about eliminating possible claimants to the throne. He also defeated the Angles and took over their territories. By 1034, the kingdoms of the Picts, the Scots, the Angles, and the Britons were united by Gaelic-speaking kings and churchmen.

THE MIDDLE AGES

Scottish kings did not follow a direct father-to-son succession but were selected from a wider pool of eligible candidates based on ancestry and political power. William Shakespeare's play *Macbeth* is a fictional account of intrigue in the medieval Scottish court. Unlike the character in the play, however, the real Macbeth was a successful and well-liked king, according to historical accounts.

King David I (who reigned 1124—1153) and later kings of Scotland increasingly adopted a social system from England and elsewhere in Europe that came to be called feudalism. Loyal followers of the king were bestowed plots of land, burghs (towns) were given royal charters for conducting specific types of business, and a military hierarchy was established to enforce royal authority.

These changes were imposed eventually upon Lowland Scotland, in part by bringing in people from northern England and the Low Countries of the Continent (Europe). In the Highlands, a kin-based social system evolved whose economy was based on the raising of cattle. As Gaelic was displaced from the

Sir William Wallace (ca. 1270–1305) is one of Scotland's greatest national heroes. A son of a knight, he fought for freedom from English rule and raised an army of lesser nobles, peasants, and townspeople, all angry at the injustices perpetrated on the Scottish people. Sir William had one successful battle with the English at Stirling Bridge in 1297, taking over Stirling Castle.

Upon his return from the battle, Sir William was knighted and named "guardian of Scotland and leader of its armies." The following year, however, his troops were wiped out by the English army at the Battle of Falkirk, and Wallace fled to France. On August 5, 1305, he was arrested near Glasgow. Wallace was taken to London, where he was condemned as a traitor to King Edward I, even though he maintained that

A statue of William Wallace stands in the National Wallace Monument in Stirling.

he had never sworn allegiance to the king. He was hanged, disemboweled, beheaded, and quartered. His mutilated body was put on display, and it was said that his quartered remains were subsequently sent to Newcastle, Berwick, Stirling, and Perth.

A monument to Wallace built in 1862 stands atop a rock on Abbey Craig, slightly north of Stirling. He is still remembered today as a patriot and national hero. In a 2002 poll conducted in the UK by the British Broadcasting Corporation (BBC), Wallace was ranked 48th in a list of the 100 greatest Britons. Wallace was portrayed by Mel Gibson in the 1995 Oscar-winning movie Braveheart.

Scottish royal court and the Lowlands, Highlanders looked increasingly toward Ireland and away from the Lowlands for cultural standards and development in the arts, literature, and culture. Two cultures thus developed in Scotland: a Gaelic-speaking and clan-based culture in the Highlands, and a feudal and mercantile-oriented society in the Lowlands, where the people spoke a form of Middle English that eventually came to be known as Scots.

In 1290, the Scottish throne fell vacant, and Edward I of England was asked to choose a successor. Out of several contenders, he chose John Balliol (ca. 1249–1314), and in exchange for his favor, Edward demanded homage from him. During John's reign, Edward made Scotland into a vassal state of England. This didn't sit well with the Scottish, and in 1295, Balliol gave up his loyalty to England and formed an alliance with France, known as the Auld Alliance.

A year later, Edward I invaded Scotland, setting off the first of the Wars of Scottish Independence. Edward deposed Balliol and imprisoned him in the infamous Tower of London. He also incurred the wrath of the Scots by removing the Stone of Destiny, used in the coronation of Scottish kings. Resistance to English rule, led by Sir William Wallace, grew.

In 1306, Robert the Bruce (Robert VIII de Bruce), also called Robert I (1274–1329), crowned himself king of Scotland. In 1314, there was a decisive battle at Bannockburn, south of Stirling, when the English troops of Edward II were defeated and driven out of Scotland by Robert's army. In 1320, Robert's supporters petitioned the pope in the Declaration of Arbroath to declare Scotland an independent nation. Eight years later, England's Edward III agreed to renounce any claims to Scotland.

MARY, QUEEN OF SCOTS, AND THE SCOTTISH REFORMATION

After independence, a few centuries of weak kings and regencies followed. The major families of Scotland again fought for power. This came to a head during the reign of Mary, Queen of Scots, who was crowned as a Catholic monarch in 1542 when she was six days old. Mary was to marry Edward, the heir of England's King Henry VIII of England, but when the Scottish regents rejected the plan, Henry VIII invaded Scotland.

The regents sought help from France, which expelled the English from Scotland. Mary was sent to France at age five and brought up in the French court. In 1558, she married the French dauphin (heir to the throne), Francis.

Mary, Queen of Scots, is pictured in an engraving by W. T. Fry. It was published in the 1823 book *Portraits of Illustrious Personages of Great Britain* by Edmund Lodge.

She returned to Scotland three years later, after the death of her husband, and found it a very different country. While she was away, religious reforms led by John Knox had taken place, and Scotland's elite had made Protestantism the official religion of the nation. Catholic mass was forbidden, and the authority of the pope was no longer recognized (even though many Catholics continued to practice their religion despite persecution). The nobles had confiscated church lands, and Knox was proposing that Scotland did not need a monarch.

As a Roman Catholic in an officially Protestant nation and as the closest heir, by descent from Henry VII's daughter, to Queen Elizabeth I of England, Mary had several enemies. In 1565, Mary married her second cousin, Henry Stuart, Lord Darnley, with whom she had a son, James. Darnley was murdered two years later. Shortly after, Mary married James Hepburn, the prime suspect in her husband's murder. In 1567, Mary was forced to abdicate in favor of her infant son, James VI, and was imprisoned in a castle on Loch Leven in central Scotland. She escaped to England and sought refuge with her cousin Elizabeth I. Fearing that Mary could be a threat to the English throne, Elizabeth imprisoned her for the next nineteen years. Mary was then found guilty of plotting to assassinate Elizabeth, and on February 8, 1587, at the age of forty-four, Mary was executed at Fotheringhay Castle in Northamptonshire, England.

THE SEVENTEENTH CENTURY

Mary's son, James VI, was raised as a Protestant. When Elizabeth I died in 1603, he succeeded her, becoming James I of England and temporarily uniting the two countries, making him one of Scotland's most successful kings. Once established in England, James passed laws bringing bishops back to the Scottish church, thus making himself more powerful, since he appointed them.

His son Charles I, however, was not as successful a king as James. He imposed the High Anglican form of worship on the Church of Scotland. This provoked thousands to sign a pledge called the National Covenant in 1638 to maintain the Presbyterian prayer service. A crisis developed, and the Covenanters recruited a huge army. Unable to muster troops of his own without money, Charles called on the English Parliament, which he hoped would agree to raise taxes for an army. Instead, it criticized Charles's rule, and in 1642, he declared war on his own Parliament. Both sides asked for the assistance of the Scottish Parliament, and it sided with the English Parliament.

The parliamentary armies, led by Oliver Cromwell, captured Charles I. He was executed by the English on January 30, 1649. However, the two allies soon fell out; the Scots wanted rule by the church, and the English wanted rule by Parliament. Cromwell invaded Scotland and seized power, and the country was ruled by commissioners established by the English Parliament.

When Charles II, a son of Charles I, was restored to the throne in 1660, he compromised with the Scottish church leaders. He reinstated the bishops and publicly advocated religious tolerance. This attitude was influenced by a belief that this would lead to a tolerance of Roman Catholicism, a religion he favored. In 1692, however, following the failure of Charles II's Declaration of Indulgence—which tried to provide civil liberties for Roman Catholics—Parliament passed the Test Act prohibiting Catholics from holding public office.

James II of England, who succeeded his father in 1685, was a Catholic. He was the victim of the wrath of the Protestants and was deposed in 1689. He was replaced by his nephew and son-in-law, William of Orange, who was a Protestant. In Scotland, the bishops were abolished again, but William was careful not to return political power to the Presbyterian Church. Control of the state thus remained with the Scottish Parliament.

THE ACTS OF UNION

Although the accession of William of Orange calmed much of the dispute between the Scottish church and the English state, things were still not resolved. William's reign was dominated by war with France, an old ally of Scotland in the latter's efforts to maintain independence. Scots fought against France in the war, which ended trade between Scotland and France. Around the same time, the Bank of England and a group of Scottish merchants formed a trading company in Panama. The venture was a disaster, and Scotland, which had to continue to pay taxes to England, nearly became bankrupt. Riots against the English broke out in Scottish towns.

Queen Anne succeeded her brother-in-law and cousin William III of England and II of Scotland. During her reign, in an attempt to preserve peace between the two countries, the English and Scottish Parliaments passed the Acts of Union in 1707. It bound England, Wales, and Scotland into the Kingdom of Great Britain. Scotland's Parliament was then combined with England's, but Scottish law and the Presbyterian Church remained the same.

The death of Queen Anne in 1714 marked the end of the Stuart monarchy. She was succeeded by her German cousin George I of Hanover. The Acts of Union had been designed to put an end to Jacobite hopes of a Stuart restoration by ensuring that the Hanoverian dynasty succeeded the childless Queen Anne upon her death. The Jacobites were a group of mostly Scottish people in the late seventeenth and eighteenth centuries who believed that the Catholic James VII of Scotland (James II of England) and his Stuart descendants should be restored to the throne of Scotland and England.

The Stuarts still commanded a lot of loyalty in Scotland, however. Thus many Scots bitterly opposed the union with England, and there were attempts known as the Jacobite Risings in 1708, 1715, 1719, and 1745 to restore the Stuart kings to the throne and release Scotland from the union with England.

The risings culminated in the Battle of Culloden in 1746 led by Charles Edward Stuart—also known as Bonnie Prince Charlie—who was the grandson of the deposed James II. As many as 1,200 Jacobites were killed, and Prince Charlie fled to France. The English government passed the Disarming Act, which banned Scots from wearing tartans and owning weapons. Those who had led the risings lost their land, and private armies were made illegal. This effectively brought the Scottish clan system to an end.

HIGHLAND CLEARANCES

For centuries, the clan system had encouraged a large population in Scotland. Clan chiefs needed large armies to fight their battles, and they rewarded their supporters with land. The end of the Jacobite Risings in 1746, however, led to the dismantling of the clan system. There was no longer a need for huge numbers of fighting men, and this led to large-scale displacements of the population of the Scottish Highlands known as the Highland Clearances. The clearances were particularly notorious because of the lack of legal protection for the evicted tenants and the abruptness of the change.

The clearances began with the introduction of sheep farming in the Highlands in 1760. The chiefs who had not had their estates confiscated no longer needed to lease their lands to tenants in order to maintain their loyalty, and soaring wool prices meant that it was more profitable to turn their lands over to sheep farming. Unfortunately, few Highlanders had the capital to acquire large flocks or experience in raising sheep. As a result, the remaining clan chiefs brought in southern sheep farmers who had both capital and experience.

A traditional thatched Hebridean cottage stands on the coast of North Uist, an island in the Outer Hebrides. It was probably built around 1750 as a home for a fisherman or crofter.

The clan chiefs, estate managers, and accountants came up with various solutions to evict the tenants still living on the lands needed for sheep farming. Some people were encouraged to emigrate; thousands of Scots went to the United States and Canada in the late eighteenth and early nineteenth centuries. Some were forced out of their land—the worst of the Highland Clearances was that by the Countess of Sutherland, who had 15,000 people brutally thrown out of their homes between 1805 and 1821. To force people to move, the roofs of their houses were often pulled down, and the trees used to build these roofs were set on fire to prevent people from rebuilding.

The early clearances pushed Highlanders from the interior to the coast, creating a new class of Scot: the crofter. Crofters were given small pieces of land, called crofts. The land that was offered was usually bad and unwanted by sheep farmers, so the crofters had to adjust to a new lifestyle and try to eke out a living through fishing and kelping while in many cases continuing to farm on their small plots of land. The crofters lived their daily lives as tenant farmers until the end of the nineteenth century, when the kelp industry collapsed and the price of cattle fell as well. There were now large numbers of people unable to pay their rents or even survive.

In response to the plight of the crofters, the Crofters' Holdings Act was passed in 1886. The act gave the crofters security of tenure, the right to arbitration when faced with rent increases, the right to bequeath their tenancies, and the right to compensation.

The Stone of Destiny (also known as the Stone of Scone) has long been accorded magical powers. One medieval legend claimed it to be the stone on which the biblical patriarch Jacob rested his head at Bethel when he dreamed of a ladder to heaven. A rectangular block of pale yellow sandstone weighing 336 pounds (152 kilograms) and measuring 26 inches (66 cm) by 16 inches (41 cm) by 11 inches (28 cm), with a Latin cross its only decoration, the stone was revered wherever it was taken. It became the coronation seat of the Scottish kings.

Edward I of England transferred the stone to Westminster Abbey in London in 1296 and placed it under the coronation throne there so that English monarchs could demonstrate their supremacy over Scotland symbolically. The stone stayed in Westminster Abbey for nearly seven hundred years.

On Christmas morning 1950, the stone was stolen by Scottish nationalists, who took it back to Scotland. Four months later, it was recovered and restored to Westminster Abbey. In 1996, however, the British government returned the stone to Scotland. Today, it is on display at Edinburgh Castle.

Or is it? According to the Westminster Stone theory, monks hid the real stone, fooling the English thieves. According to legend, the real Stone of Destiny is still hidden and will be returned by its guardians when the time is right.

A replica of the Stone of Destiny is on display on Moot Hill.

THE INDUSTRIAL REVOLUTION

From the 1820s, the Industrial Revolution was in full swing in Scotland. From a rural, agricultural economy, Scotland was propelled into the modern, capitalist world through scientific and technological breakthroughs, evolving into a country of huge towns, massive factories, and heavy industry.

Similar to that of the rest of Britain, Scotland's Industrial Revolution depended on the trade of American and West Indian cotton and tobacco. Glasgow was particularly suited to this trade, being located on the west coast of Scotland. The journey to America was convenient, and there was a large pool of people to provide a workforce, many of them having recently been turned out of their homes during the Highland Clearances. A cotton-processing industry developed with mass-production techniques in large factories.

The need for mechanization encouraged the iron industry, which in turn fueled the coal industry. Scotland had plenty of iron and coal. Trade fostered a shipbuilding industry, as steam-driven ships were developed. The population drifted toward the centers of industry in the Lowlands. Glasgow grew rapidly, leading to the development of urban overcrowding in tenement buildings with poor sanitation. The Irish, fleeing from famine, swelled the urban population. Many workers, such as coal miners, suffered terrible hardships with no organized labor movements to protect them and no right to vote.

In the early part of the nineteenth century, several attempts to organize the workers ended in mass arrests and deportations to Australia. In 1832, the Reform Bill (also known as the Great Reform Act) was passed, giving middle-class people the right to vote. The act also granted extra seats in the House of Commons to larger towns and cities that had expanded significantly during the Industrial Revolution. Those seeking fairer voting rights welcomed the passage of the act. It represented an important shift of power from aristocratic and landed interests to the growing urban middle classes. Little improvement was made in the well-being of the poor, however. The act was criticized for enfranchising only the "respectable" classes. There was no secret ballot, and landowning interests continued to hold an important sway over new voters. Many unskilled laborers were unable to vote until 1918.

WORLD WARS I AND II

World War I had a devastating effect on Scottish society. Thousands of Scots were killed fighting in Europe, and the prosperity of Scottish industry was damaged. Trade with America stopped. The shipbuilding industry, in particular, did not recover from the effects of changing trade patterns. Scotland suffered

Shipworkers rivet steel plates together for the keel of a new aircraft carrier for the Royal Navy at John Brown & Company shipyard at Clydebank in 1939, shortly after the outbreak of World War II.

some of the worst social conditions in the UK. This led to the highest infant mortality rate in Europe. The distress bred political radicalism. Socialist groups grew in strength, and twenty-two members of the Scottish Labor Party were elected to Parliament in 1922.

As the world entered the economic slump of the 1930s, Scotland continued to suffer badly, and emigration to America increased. Some four hundred thousand Scots—10 percent of the population—left the country between 1921 and 1931. By 1936, the annual output of the shipyards had fallen from 826,560 tons (749,843 metric tons) to less than 59,040 tons (53,560 metric tons). Two-thirds of the workforce was unemployed. In this atmosphere of poverty and depression, in 1934, the Scottish National Party (SNP) was formed.

World War II put an end to the economic depression in Scotland. The shipbuilding industry revived, stimulating coal mining and other war-related industries. The shipyards in the Glasgow area, called Clydeside, started construction on warships, and engineering firms began making arms and ammunition. The west-central region of Scotland became indispensable. Aware of this fact, the Germans bombed Clydeside on March 13 and 14, 1941, killing 1,000 people and injuring 1,500.

Otherwise, however, Scotland prospered until World War II ended, when demand for ships and armaments stopped. In the following years, Scotland benefited, along with the rest of Britain, from the massive social changes taking place. Free health care reduced the infant mortality rate, education improved, privately owned industries were nationalized, and a massive rebuilding program began. Like the rest of Britain, though, Scotland experienced competition from newly emerging countries, and Scottish industry declined until the discovery of North Sea oil in the 1970s. The find resurrected the economy and provided jobs for thousands.

By the end of the 1970s, the old industries of Scotland were stagnant, and more and more people began to believe that Scotland's future lay in independence. In a 1979 referendum, 52 percent of the Scots who voted were in favor of devolution. In this case, that meant the creation of a Scottish legislature, with the responsibilities of government divided between the new assembly and the UK government. Many saw this as a step toward Scottish independence. However, the measure did not pass.

THE SCOTTISH PARLIAMENT

Scotland benefited little during the 1980s, when Conservative leader Margaret Thatcher was the prime minister of England. The Scots remembered that they had once formed a powerful, independent nation, and nationalistic sentiments grew. After the 1992 elections, only a small number of Scottish Conservative Party members were in the British Parliament, and once again, Scotland found itself ruled by a government it largely had not elected. This further fueled the country's sense of alienation.

In 1997, the Labour Party won a landslide victory in the general elections that saw the Conservatives lose all their Scottish seats and the Scottish National Party (SNP), which favors independence, win six seats in Parliament. Led by Prime Minister Tony Blair, the Labour government in England called a referendum for devolution and the establishment of a Scottish Parliament with a broad range of powers, including control over the country's health and education systems. The referendum garnered more than 74 percent of votes in favor of the process. Devolution was finally taking place.

In May 1999, Scotland held its own parliamentary elections for the first time in three hundred years. Devolution has allowed Scotland to develop distinctive policies, including financial support for students and land reform.

INDEPENDENCE AT LAST?

In 2014, Scotland held a historic referendum, asking the Scottish people, "Should Scotland be an independent country?" Leading up to the referendum, the SNP had become the largest party in the Scottish Parliament, led by First Minister Alex Salmond. The SNP had run on the promise to hold such a referendum. The party initiated a "National Conversation" in 2007, during which the country explored the ramifications of declaring independence from the United Kingdom. The issues involved with disentangling itself from the UK—economic, financial, defense, energy, and not least, membership in the European Union—were complicated.

The campaign prior to the vote was vigorous, with both sides earning strong public support. Campaigning on behalf of independence was the group Yes Scotland, along with other groups; campaigning on behalf of remaining in the UK was the group Better Together, backed by the Conservative Party, Labour Party, and Liberal Democrats.

Meanwhile, the UK government, under Prime Minister David Cameron, stated that it wished for Scotland to remain in the UK, but it would go along with the will of the Scottish people.

The voting age for the referendum was lowered from eighteen to sixteen. The turnout on the day of the vote was very high, with 84.6 percent of the Scottish electorate participating. In the end, the "no" vote won the day, with 55.3 percent voting against independence and 44.7 percent voting for it.

In the aftermath, contrary to what might be expected, the SNP picked up thousands of new members and became even stronger in the Scottish Parliament. In a sign of possible conflict ahead, the United Kingdom in 2016 held a UK-wide referendum on European Union (EU) membership, which had been a hot issue for some years prior. The UK had been a member of the EU since 1973. In the referendum, the majority of UK voters chose to leave the EU, 52 to 48 percent. This movement to leave the EU came to be dubbed "Brexit." However, Scotland voted overwhelmingly to remain in the EU, 62 to 38 percent. Of the four constituent countries in the UK, England and Wales voted to leave, while Northern Ireland and Scotland voted to remain, with Scotland's vote being by far the more lopsided. However, England accounts for 84 percent of the UK's population—Scotland a mere 8 percent—so the will of the English carried the day.

With the election in 2019 of the highly controversial English politician Boris Johnson as prime minister of the United Kingdom, many Scottish people began calling once again for another referendum on independence. One reason was Johnson's hard push for a "no-deal" Brexit. (A no-deal Brexit would entail leaving the EU and all its institutions without any agreements in place for what would occur in the aftermath. It would also take place without a transition period to give the UK a chance to negotiate new trade agreements in lieu of the previous EU deals.)

Another concern is that the prime minister has, in the past, publicly stated anti-Scottish views. In 2005, for example, Johnson called for Scottish people to be blocked from becoming prime minister because "government by a Scot is just not conceivable." Also, when he was the editor of the *Spectator*, a news magazine, he published (though did not himself write) an apparently satirical poem describing Scottish people as "a verminous race" who were "polluting our stock" and should be exterminated.

INTERNET LINKS

https://www.ancient.eu/scotland
The ancient history of Scotland is covered on this site.

http://www.bbc.co.uk/scotland/history/articles
The BBC offers a series of articles about Scottish history.

https://www.scotland.org/about-scotland/history-timeline
This travel site includes a brief timeline of Scottish history.

https://whc.unesco.org/en/list/430
The World Heritage listing for Frontiers of the Roman Empire discusses the Antonine Wall and Hadrian's Wall ruins in Great Britain.

https://whc.unesco.org/en/list/514
The World Heritage listing for the Heart of Neolithic Orkney explores the Neolithic monuments on Orkney Island.

GOVERNMENT

The Scottish Parliament Building, or Holyrood, is in Edinburgh.

3

SCOTLAND HAS PARTIAL SELF-government within the United Kingdom and representation in the UK Parliament. While the UK is based in London, the Scottish government is based in Edinburgh. It has powers over matters pertaining to the economy, education, health, justice, rural affairs, housing, environment, equal opportunities, consumer advocacy and advice, transport, and taxation. The UK government, meanwhile, reserves the power to oversee immigration, the constitution, foreign policy, and defense.

The Scottish Parliament is located in the Holyrood section of the capital city, Edinburgh. Therefore, the Parliament itself is often referred to as Holyrood, in much the same way that the UK government is called Westminster and the US government is often referred to as Washington.

UNION WITH ENGLAND

In 1707, the Acts of Union combined the Kingdom of England (which had united with Wales in 1536) and the Kingdom of Scotland. At the time, they were separate states with separate legislatures but the same monarch. According to the treaty, the two kingdoms were "United into One Kingdom by the Name of Great Britain." The move was much to England's advantage and was largely opposed by the Scottish people, who held sometimes violent demonstrations against the union.

Scotland was in a very weak position to resist, however. Its attempt to establish a colony in Panama in the late 1690s had left it bankrupt. The colony, Caledonia, was an attempt to make Scotland into a world trading power by virtue of its location on the shortest overland route from the Atlantic to the Pacific Ocean. The colony was a disaster—most of the settlers died—and was abandoned after just a few years. At that point, the wealthy members of Scottish society decided it would be better for them to hitch their personal fortunes to the economy of the much more successful England, and the Scottish Parliament was dissolved.

DEVOLUTION

In the twentieth century, responsibility for Scotland was gradually handed over to the Scottish Office, whose headquarters was moved from London to Edinburgh in 1939. The office was headed by the secretary of state for Scotland, who was a member of the British cabinet. In the 1960s, talk began of a devolved government for Scotland, but a referendum held in 1979 did not gather the 40 percent plurality required for this to take place.

The change came in 1997 with the election of a new Labour government in Britain committed to devolution—devolution is a shift in power to a lower level, in this case to local government—in both Scotland and Wales. Its proposal for Scotland was a limited form of self-government with a Parliament empowered to legislate in such areas as education, agriculture, health, and justice, and to levy taxes. A referendum was held in 1997: 74.3 percent voted for the establishment of the Scottish Parliament, and 53.5 percent of the voters were in favor of regaining the power to levy and vary taxes. Scotland elected its own Parliament in 1999 for the first time in three hundred years. Further powers were devolved to the Parliament by the Scotland Act of 2012 and the Scotland Act of 2016.

THE MONARCH

As Scotland is still part of the United Kingdom, the British monarch is the head of state, the head of the judiciary, and the commander in chief of the armed forces. Since 1953, this has been Queen Elizabeth II (b. 1926), and her heir apparent is Charles, Prince of Wales (b. 1948). All acts of the Parliament require the queen's assent, and it is she who confers peerages and other honors. These are largely technicalities and are carried out by the government in London with Queen Elizabeth's consent. The queen lives for part of the year at Balmoral Castle in northeastern Scotland.

PARLIAMENT

The Scottish Parliament is a unicameral legislature. This means there is only one legislative, or lawmaking, chamber. It consists of 129 members who are referred to as "Members of the Scottish Parliament" (MSPs). Seventy-three of the MSPs are chosen from single-member constituencies, and fifty-six are elected by proportional representation from regional party lists. The leading parliamentary party appoints the Scottish executive branch, which is led by a first minister.

Queen Elizabeth II attends the official opening ceremony of the Queensferry Crossing on September 4, 2017, in South Queensferry, Scotland. The bridge crosses the Firth of Forth near Edinburgh and is the world's longest three-tower, cable-stayed bridge.

The two-part system for choosing MSPs differs from the system used in the rest of Britain. The first seventy-three MSPs are chosen using the traditional system of elections in the UK, called the first-past-the-post system. This means whoever gets the most votes wins. The use of proportional representation for the remaining MSPs is unique to Scotland. Essentially, this type of voting aims to allocate elected MSPs in proportion to the total votes cast for a particular political party within a region. Every voter effectively has two votes, one for a constituency representative and the other for regional representatives.

LOCAL GOVERNMENT

Local authorities in Scotland are administrative bodies. They are required to act within the framework of laws passed by the European, UK, and Scottish Parliaments. They are responsible for community services that include environmental matters, urban planning, education, sanitation, and elections. Scotland is divided into thirty-two council areas, each administered by a local council. These council areas vary in both geographical extent and population. The largest council area is Highland, encompassing 12,552 square miles (32,518 sq km), whereas the most populous council area is Glasgow, with a population of about 608,000. Within each local council area are hundreds of communities, including towns, villages, and city neighborhoods.

THE JUDICIARY

At the union of Scotland and England in 1707, Scottish law was allowed to remain independent, so Scotland has always had its own set of laws and judicial system based on Roman law with Celtic influences. One way in which the Scottish legal system differs from the English is that the age of legal capacity, or legal adulthood, is sixteen, whereas in England it is eighteen. Another difference is that at the end of a trial the verdict can be "guilty," "not guilty," or "not proven." The last is known as the "Scotch verdict."

The royal coat of arms marks the facade of the High Court of Justiciary in Glasgow.

UNITED KINGDOM FLAGS

England

Scotland

Wales

Northern Ireland

The UK flag is the flag of Britain, popularly called the Union Jack. The red, white, and blue design features a combination of the flags of England and Scotland. The red-and-white Saint George's cross, representing the patron saint of England, is laid over the blue-and-white Saint Andrew's cross, honoring the patron saint and flag of Scotland. The Union Jack also incorporates the flag of Saint Patrick, patron saint of Ireland, even though the Republic of Ireland is no longer part of the United Kingdom. Northern Ireland, however, remains in the UK.

The flag of Scotland is called the Saltire, or the Saint Andrew's Cross. It features a diagonal white cross—two white bands crisscrossing from corner to corner—against a blue background. The tone of blue has varied over the years, and in 2003, the Scottish government adopted Pantone 300 as the official blue.

The official animal of Scotland is the unicorn, and the flower is the thistle, a bristly plant with a purple blossom. The two are featured in the Scottish coat of arms, in which two crowned unicorns rear up in a field of thistles.

The motto of Scotland is "In My Defens God Me Defend" ("defens" = defense).

The ministers responsible for judicial affairs are the lord advocate and the solicitor general (akin to the attorney general in the United States). They give advice to the Scottish government on legal matters and help to formulate legislation.

In Scotland, the most serious criminal cases, involving murder, rape, and grave drug offenses, are tried in the High Court of Justiciary. Civil cases that involve challenging government decisions are heard in the Court of Session. The Court of Session, which is made up of the lord president, the lord justice clerk, and twenty-two other judges, is divided into the Inner House and the Outer House. Minor civil and criminal cases are heard in the sheriff courts and the district courts.

POLITICAL PARTIES

Scotland has four major political parties and several smaller ones. For many years, the Labour Party had been the strongest party in Scotland. As of 2019, though, the Scottish National Party (SNP) is the front-runner. Similar to the British government, in Scotland it is the national parties that retain overall command of budgetary policies. Now that devolution has occurred, there is much debate over Scotland's constitutional status and whether Scotland should accrue additional powers in areas such as fiscal policy or seek to obtain full independence and sovereign powers.

THE SCOTTISH NATIONAL PARTY   is a center-left nationalist political party. Founded in 1934, it is committed to Scottish independence. The SNP has had continuous representation in the British Parliament since 1967 but tended to fare poorly in UK general elections. Immediately after devolution, the SNP polled the second-highest number of votes in Scotland. This, however, has changed. By allying with a smaller party, the SNP gained control of the government in 2007, and Alex Salmond became first minister. It won an outright majority in the next election, in 2011, and has continued to dominate since.

Under Salmond, the party held the referendum on independence in 2014, which failed to pass. Following the defeat, Salmond resigned and Nicola Sturgeon, also of the SNP, became the first minister of the Scottish Parliament.

THE SCOTTISH LABOUR PARTY was founded in January 1976 as a breakaway from the British Labour Party by members who were dissatisfied with the failure of the UK Labour government to secure a devolved Scottish assembly. Historically, it was the largest political party in modern Scottish politics, having dominated the country's political scene for several decades. In 2007, however, it became the country's second-largest party, with a lower share of the vote and one fewer parliamentary seat than the SNP. The Labour Party's policies are dubbed a "third way;" it supposedly avoids the class-ridden party politics characteristic of British politics. It was responsible for initiating devolution for Scotland in 1997.

THE CONSERVATIVE PARTY (officially the Scottish Conservative and Unionist Party) was established in 1965. The referendums for devolution and independence were opposed by the Conservatives.

THE SCOTTISH LIBERAL DEMOCRATS campaigned for the creation of a devolved Scottish Parliament. This party believes that the Parliament should exercise more responsibility over fiscal matters.

INTERNET LINKS

https://www.gov.scot
This is the official site of the Scottish government.

https://www.gov.uk
**https://www.gov.uk/government/organisations/office-of-the
-secretary-of-state-for-scotland**
The top URL links to the official site of the UK government, and the bottom URL links to the page for the secretary of state for Scotland.

**https://www.visitscotland.com/about/uniquely-scottish/national
-animal-unicorn**
This travel site explains why the unicorn is the symbol of Scotland.

ECONOMY

Wildflowers bloom on the hillside around Edinburgh Castle.

4

SCOTLAND'S ECONOMY IS CLOSELY associated with that of England and the rest of the United Kingdom. Most of Scotland's trade has been within the UK and the European Union (EU), though the 2016 vote to leave the EU has since jeopardized the latter.

From the time of the Industrial Revolution (approximately 1760—1840) through the late twentieth century, Scotland's economy was dominated by heavy industry. It was primarily supported by shipbuilding in Glasgow, as well as the coal mining and steel industries. The decline of these industries during the 1970s and 1980s, however, led to a fundamental change in the nature of the Scottish economy. Unemployment became a serious problem, and successive governments made efforts to improve conditions. During the 1980s, Scotland's economy benefited enormously from the discovery of North Sea petroleum and natural gas.

Though Scotland's economy is small, as of late 2019, it was thriving. It accounted for about 5 percent of the UK's export income, and unemployment was low, at 3.6 percent. Scotland's GDP per capita was higher than in any other part of the UK, except for London. Traditional industries such as woolen and tweed production and whisky (the Scottish spelling of whiskey) distilling continue to do well.

Gross domestic product (GDP) is a measure of a country's total production. The number reflects the total value of goods and services produced over one year. Economists use it to determine whether a country's economy is growing or contracting. Growth is good, while a falling GDP means trouble. Dividing the GDP by the number of people in the country determines the GDP per capita (per person). This number provides an indication of a country's average standard of living—the higher the better.

In 2018, the GDP per capita in Scotland was estimated to be $43,740 (though sources differ). That figure would have ranked Scotland about 42nd out of 228 countries listed by the CIA World Factbook. *However the* Factbook *only lists the UK GDP per capita as a whole; it was $44,300. For comparison, the United States that year was number 19, with a GDP per capita of $59,800. Ireland came in at a high 10th place, with $73,200.*

HEAVY INDUSTRY

The manufacturing and the construction industries contribute about 25 percent of Scotland's annual gross domestic product (GDP). Heavy industry, however, has declined. During the country's period of industrial prosperity in the early twentieth century, shipbuilding, coal mining, steel production, and engineering transformed the Central Lowlands into the world's most heavily industrialized area. Glasgow was the center of activity, and Glaswegians called it the "second city in the empire." Industries in Glasgow and its satellite towns produced one-fifth of Britain's steel, one-third of its shipping tonnage, half of its marine horsepower, a third of its railroads' rolling stock, and almost all its sewing machines.

Similar to other manufacturing areas, Scotland's cities suffered as technology changed and big engineering projects became rarer. The steel industry became less profitable and closed down, whereas reserves of coal declined until working the mines became unprofitable. Only opencast mining is carried out in Scotland now. A boom in the engineering industry came when oil was discovered in the North Sea, and several Scottish firms developed new skills in oil-rig manufacturing that have been used both off the coast of Scotland and abroad.

OFFSHORE OIL AND GAS

Scotland has a flourishing energy industry thanks to an abundance of natural resources. While coal was once Scotland's main natural resource and a leading factor in the industrialization of the country, most of the accessible coal resources are now inoperative. In 1913, peak production stood at 50.7 million tons (46 million metric tons) per year.

Other natural resources that have been mined commercially at various times include gold, silver, dolomite, granite, and chromite, but these are not mined in large enough quantities today to maintain the industries. Peat, another valuable resource, is used domestically for fuel in the Highlands. It is not mined commercially, though, as it takes a lot of time and effort to cut and dry the peat.

The discovery of North Sea oil and its subsequent production had a stimulating effect on the economy of Scotland. The development of oil exploration led to the development of towns and service industries close to the oil fields, particularly in Aberdeen. It is estimated that the oil industry employs close to one hundred thousand people, or 6 percent of Scotland's working population.

A study published in 2019 suggested there could be 17 billion barrels of oil (or the equivalent gas) still to be extracted by 2050, in addition to the more than 43 billion barrels recovered since the 1970s. Meanwhile, oil from the Clair Ridge site, west of Shetland, began to flow at the end of 2018. That field is expected to remain productive for the next four decades. In addition, the energy firm Total announced a major gas discovery in the North Sea in 2019, the biggest find in a decade.

Scotland is now Europe's leading offshore oil and gas producer, but the government set a target of 50 percent of electricity to be generated through renewable sources of power by 2020. The country ended up exceeding that goal, generating 74.6 percent of its electricity from renewable sources in 2018.

ELECTRONICS

Scotland has a small but growing electronics and microelectronics industry in the region between Glasgow and Edinburgh, known as Silicon Glen (the name

BREXIT: A COMPLICATED BREAKUP

As part of the United Kingdom, Scotland had been part of the European Union since 1973. In the twenty-first century, however, many people in Britain grew dissatisfied with the EU, and for complicated reasons, they began to discuss quitting, or exiting, the organization—a move that came to be called Brexit.

A referendum in 2016 saw the "leave" vote win by 51.9 percent. Some of the factors thought to be behind the majority vote were a desire to beef up British sovereignty and the need to control the influx of immigrants. Many voters felt that EU membership took decision-making away from the British people and that EU regulatory bodies held dominion over the nation. In addition, they (somewhat erroneously) blamed the heavy influx of immigrants to the UK in recent years on EU policies.

The "stay" voters, meanwhile, pointed to the economic benefits of membership—a common economic market and the advantages of globalization. In general, the "leave" voter was older and less educated. Younger, more educated voters were more inclined to vote "stay." One factor that might have swayed the results is that older voters turned out in greater numbers for the referendum than did younger ones.

In Scotland, however, the vote was heavily in favor of remaining in the EU, but the Scottish factor was not enough to influence the overall outcome. Therefore, Scotland was left trying to figure out how Brexit would influence its economy and what, if anything, could be done about it.

The SNP, holding a majority in the Scottish government, expected Brexit to impose long-term damage on the Scottish economy, shrinking its GDP by up to 7 percent and decreasing Scottish exports by 10 to 20 percent. The resulting economic slowdown would likely increase the unemployment rate to 8 percent, slashing one hundred thousand Scottish jobs, and Scottish citizens would see their real disposable income drop by almost 10 percent. In addition, the SNP predicted other calamities that would affect various sectors of everyday life.

Scotland's preferred option was to hold a second referendum. At this writing in late 2019, the situation remained up in the air.

is inspired by the name Silicon Valley in California, a tech innovation hub in the United States). Today, many international tech companies have a presence in Silicon Glen, including Microsoft, Amazon, Adobe Systems, Motorola, Oracle, and Toshiba.

Software, and in particular gaming, is a big growth industry, as is space technology. Eighteen percent of the UK's space industry is based in Scotland, and Glasgow builds more satellites than any other city in Europe.

FINANCE

Scotland is Europe's fifth-largest financial center, and it is home to influential financial players such as the Bank of Scotland, the Royal Bank of Scotland, Clydesdale Bank, Scottish Widows, and Standard Life. This industry has grown greatly in the twenty-first century, with a growth rate of 35 percent from 2000 to 2005 alone. The finance sector accounts for about one hundred thousand jobs and generates 7 percent of the country's GDP. Among the main banking and insurance jobs are legal and computer services, accountancy, and property services. Since the mid-1960s, Edinburgh has become an important financial and business center, second in the UK only to London.

FISHING

Fishing is an important part of Scotland's economy, but its future is uncertain with the coming of Brexit. Under EU regulations, many fishermen felt hampered by the restrictions on catches as well as by declining fish stocks in Scottish waters. Because there were fishing quotas for each vessel, fishermen had to throw away any excess fish they caught. (The EU restrictions were aimed at preventing overfishing as well as managing the overall industry.) A fisheries police force enforced these quotas, and ships have often been boarded for inspection.

Therefore, the Scottish Fishermen's Federation (SFF), a lobby group, supported Brexit. However, the post-Brexit fishing arrangements have yet to be negotiated, and many fishermen are concerned that they will be left

One of several industries that have been historically associated with Scotland is Harris Tweed. A tweed is a woven woolen textile, and Harris Island in the Outer Hebrides is where this industry got its start in the nineteenth century. (The word "tweed" derives from tweel, *a Scots word for "twill," which is a certain kind of woven pattern. In 1830, a London merchant misread the word "tweel" as "tweed," as in the River Tweed, and the name stuck.)*

Harris Tweed is a 100 percent wool woven fabric used primarily in men's jackets, but also in other clothing and goods, including handbags and shoes. Production of the cloth began as a cottage industry in the Outer Hebrides. The tweed was handmade by fishermen's wives in their homes from the wool of the sheep they reared themselves. The wool was washed, dyed, spun, and "waulked," or made soft by beating it on a table, by one woman and her family or friends.

Over the years, the high quality of the material came to be synonymous with the name Harris Tweed, and the name became protected by Scottish law in 1993. Only true Harris Tweed can be labeled with the Orb trademark, guaranteeing its authenticity. According to an official statement, "Harris Tweed ... has been hand woven by the islanders at their homes in the Outer Hebrides, finished in the islands of Harris, Lewis, North Uist, Benbecula, South Uist and Barra ... and made from pure virgin wool dyed and spun in the Outer Hebrides."

out of whatever future benefits accrue from the changes. Nevertheless, the future will not mean the end of quotas, as the UK imposes its own.

Two-thirds of the British catch comes from ships registered and operating in Scottish ports. The bulk of fish brought into these ports are whitefish, including cod, haddock, and sole, as well as herring and mackerel. Peterhead, in northeast Scotland, is the European Union's largest and busiest whitefish port, and the

Grampian region of Scotland is one of Britain's main fish-processing centers. The Scottish fish-processing industry accounts for 49 percent of the UK's fish.

Shellfish are also part of an important industry in Scotland, and scallops, lobsters, langoustines, and crabs are major sources of income. They are caught in the wild and raised on fish farms. The chief areas for shellfish farming are in the Highlands and on the islands.

AGRICULTURE

About sixty-seven thousand people are employed in agriculture, about 8 percent of the rural workforce. After service and public sector jobs, agriculture is the third-largest employer in rural Scotland. The country's farmers, crofters, and growers produce goods worth around $3.52 billion a year, contributing to much of Scotland's food and drink exports.

In the Southern Uplands and the Highlands, sheep farming dominates, whereas in the southwest, with better-drained and more-accessible lands, dairy farming is more important. The eastern seaboard supports the farming of barley, potatoes, rapeseed, wheat, and oats. Silage and hay, as well as root vegetables, are produced as animal feed.

Areas in the north of Scotland—such as Argyle and Bute in the western Grampians, the Outer Hebrides, and the Orkney and Shetland Islands—are dominated by tiny farms known as crofts. Few farmers can make a living from their crofts alone; the scale of croft holdings was made intentionally small by nineteenth-century legislation that forced the holders to take seasonal work. As a consequence, many crofts have been abandoned.

FORESTRY

Forestry is a significant activity, and it has helped retain the population in the country's rural areas. These forests are maintained by Forestry Commission Scotland and private landowners, including forestry companies. Both natural woodland and planted pine forests are maintained and expanded, and timber provides significant income for the country. In fact, Scotland is responsible for about half of the UK's timber production. The European Union has designated some Highland forests as class 1 habitats, meaning that they must be protected and developed as habitats for wildlife.

OTHER INDUSTRIES

Other industries in Scotland that have contributed significantly to the national economy are traditional enterprises such as whisky and tweed manufacturing. The tourism industry is one of the biggest revenue earners.

DISTILLING   Whisky is one of Scotland's best-known manufactured exports, and the distilling industry has always been a part of Scottish economic life. It provides forty-two thousand jobs, and in 2018, exports were worth $5.7 billion, accounting for 21 percent of the value of all UK food and drink exports. It is one of the UK's top five manufactured export earners. Ninety percent of the production is exported to the United States, Japan, and the European Union.

The types of whisky produced in Scotland are malt, grain, or blended. In the first, malted barley is used, whereas in the second, a mixture of ordinary barley and other grains is used. Most Scotch whisky available is the third type, made from a blend of malt and grain whiskies. The principal whisky-producing areas are Speyside and the island of Islay. The whisky industry is closely linked to tourism, as many of these distilleries are popular tourist attractions. Well-known whisky brands from Scotland include Chivas Regal, Bell's, Teacher's, and Johnnie Walker.

TOURISM   Scotland's tourism industry employs about 207,000 people, accounting for about 7 percent of the country's employment. Edinburgh is second only to London as a tourist destination in Britain. Most of Scotland's tourists come from other countries in Britain or other parts of Scotland itself for the winter sports or the abundance of walking trails and other outdoor sports. There are more than 14 million foreign and domestic tourists visiting Scotland each year, of which about 2.8 million are from abroad—notably from the United States, Germany, France, Canada, and Australia. Those visitors bring in about 5 percent of the country's GDP, and tourist spending is valued at more than $1.49 billion each year. Some of the more popular attractions are

Scotland's rural parklands, the cultural institutions of Edinburgh and Glasgow, the Palace of Holyroodhouse, and the country's many castles.

MINERALS Scotland also produces some minerals in small amounts. Marble is quarried in the northwest, and barite is mined in the Highlands. The central belt of Scotland holds a wide variety of minerals. It is host to the UK's most productive coalfield, a third of the UK's igneous rock collieries, and significant deposits of sand, clay, and gravel. Metals, particularly lead and silver, have been produced in South Lanarkshire.

INTERNET LINKS

https://www.gov.scot/economy
The Scottish government site has detailed, up-to-date information on the economy.

https://www.harristweed.org
The home site of Harris Tweed includes history and personal stories.

https://www.insider.co.uk/all-about/scottish-tourism-industry
News and statistics about Scotland's tourism industry are available on this site.

https://www.nfus.org.uk
NFU (National Farmers Union) Scotland covers the agricultural industry.

https://www.sff.co.uk
The Scottish Fishermen's Federation covers the fishing industry.

ENVIRONMENT

A gray seal poses on a rock on an island off the Scottish coast.

5

SCOTLAND IS A HAVEN OF environmental cleanliness, beauty, wilderness, and romance. Plants and animals that cannot be found in the rest of Britain continue to exist in the rural areas of Scotland. Unfortunately, Scotland has not been spared the devastating effects of climate change, and the government is determined to play its part in rising to this challenge.

Scotland has a rich and diverse environment. It is home to a large variety of habitats and species. The east coast boasts the largest breeding colony of seals in the world and supports the breeding colony of the *Halichoerus grypus*, or gray seal. Scotland is also an internationally significant nesting ground for a variety of seabirds, such as the gannet.

Scotland's environment is important to its economy, as it generates income both directly, through farming and forestry, as well as indirectly, through tourism. Visitors from all over the world travel to Scotland to enjoy the beauty of its landscape, which encompasses vast lochs, rivers, and mountains. Protecting the environment, therefore, has been a priority for the Scottish government.

In 1995, the Scottish Environment Protection Agency (SEPA), a nondepartmental public body, was established. Sponsored by the government, SEPA is the country's environmental regulator, and it is responsible for the protection of the natural environment of Scotland.

Scotland is committed to being a world leader in the fight against climate change and is working to fight the crisis at a faster rate than the United Kingdom in general. Helped by the removal of its coal-fired power stations and its promotion of onshore wind farms, by 2019, Scotland had already cut emissions by 49 percent since 1990—a greater decrease than the UK had accomplished as a whole.

SEPA has identified several areas that can be improved upon, such as air quality, water environment, and biodiversity. It protects and improves the environment by advising ministers, regulated businesses, and industry, and by helping the public understand their environmental responsibilities. While it operates at arm's length, SEPA is still accountable through Scottish ministers to the Scottish Parliament.

CLIMATE CHANGE

First Minister Nicola Sturgeon declared a "climate emergency" in 2019—a year that saw record wildfires and unprecedented high temperatures. Dozens of towns and cities across the UK had already declared a climate emergency. While there is no single definition of what a climate emergency declaration means, many people interpret it as a declaration of becoming carbon neutral by 2030. "Carbon neutral" or having "zero carbon footprint" are terms that mean achieving no net release of carbon dioxide into the atmosphere, especially through offsetting emissions by planting trees. At the time of Sturgeon's announcement, Scotland had the goal of being carbon neutral by 2050. New targets were being set to achieve the goal by 2045.

Climate change is one of the most serious concerns facing society in the twenty-first century, and although Scotland's environment is generally one of good quality, it is undeniable that the country is already feeling the effects, with rising temperatures and more frequent winter storms. The government has agreed that if left unchecked, climate change will accelerate, causing further damage to Scotland's environment. In this aspect, it should be noted that the Scottish Parliament unanimously passed the world-leading Climate Change (Scotland) Act in 2009.

The United Kingdom, as part of the EU, is a signatory of the 1997 Kyoto Protocol and the 2015 Paris Agreement. These international treaties bring all nations together to work toward combating climate change and adapting to its effects. The key aim of the Paris Agreement is to keep the global temperature rise this century to well below 3.6°F (2°C) above pre-industrial levels and to pursue efforts to limit the temperature increase to 2.7°F (1.5°C). As of September 2019, 185 parties have ratified the Paris Agreement. (The United States ratified the agreement in 2016 under President Barack Obama. President Donald Trump, however, announced in 2017 that the United States would withdraw from the agreement. According to Article 28 of the agreement, the process will not become effective until November 4, 2020.)

AIR QUALITY

Air quality is generally good in Scotland, with the country implementing tighter limits than the rest of the UK for air pollutants. In twenty-one locations across twelve council areas, however, air quality is still poor. Poor air quality reduces life expectancy and harms human health. It also damages soils, plants, and water. The main cause of this problem is road transportation. Because of a lack of coordination between transportation and air-quality objectives at the national and local levels, in February 2009, the government issued revised guidelines to local councils, encouraging them to work with transportation and planning departments to develop air-quality strategies and action plans.

Bottlenose dolphins jump in the waters of the Moray Firth. Behind them stands Fort George, a large eighteenth-century fortress near Inverness.

THE WATER ENVIRONMENT

Scotland's marine environment is generally good. About 97 percent of Scotland's coastal waters are in good or excellent condition, but there are local impacts from commercial fishing, aquaculture, and diffuse pollution. There are concerns that growth in industries such as aquaculture and renewable energy may increase pressure on coastal waters.

Scotland has more than two thousand rivers, three hundred lochs, and 43,973 square miles (113,890 sq km) of groundwater, as well as nearly 20,000 square miles (51,800 sq km) of coastal and estuarine water. The quality of these waters is important because key Scottish industries such as whisky production and agriculture are dependent on them. In addition, improving water quality contributes to improving the biodiversity of the water environment.

Pollution from agricultural sources has been identified as the leading threat to the environment, and SEPA continues to work with land managers to address this. The good news is that water quality in Scotland has improved significantly. More than half of the country's waters meet the European standard of good ecological status. This means that more than half of Scotland's waters are only slightly different from what they would be in their natural state and can be used for drinking water and activities such as fishing. However, SEPA aims to ensure that nearly all of Scotland's waters meet this standard by 2027.

BIODIVERSITY

Biodiversity describes the variety of species that exist and the habitats they depend on. Loss of biodiversity occurs when there is a destruction of habitats, pollution, the arrival of nonnative species, and climate change. Scotland's biodiversity objectives are linked to European and UK priorities. In 2004, the European Union set out to stop the loss of biodiversity across Europe by 2010. It identified more than one thousand plant and animal species and more than two hundred habitats to be protected.

There are more than 26,000 protected areas in Europe, and 385 of these are in Scotland, forming about 20 percent of the land area. There has been mixed progress in protecting and improving Scotland's biodiversity. The government's goal of having 95 percent of all protected areas in favorable condition by 2010 was not achieved, as only 75 percent of elements such as number of species, habitats, and rock formations in protected areas are in a favorable condition. The aim to increase the number of terrestrial breeding birds, on the other hand, has been met.

SCOTLAND'S FLOWERS

Wildflowers are a fundamental part of Scotland's culture and history. Flowers that are rare or extinct in other parts of Britain, such as the ghost orchid, can still be found in Scotland. Nevertheless, one in four species of wildflower has come under threat in recent times. The flowers most at risk are the corn marigold, the heath cudweed, and the butterfly orchid. Significant declines are taking place particularly in the uplands and on farmlands. It has been estimated that each county loses one wildflower species each year. Although several conservation groups, including Plantlife Scotland, continue to work toward saving endangered plant species, places that are home to legally protected plants are still not protected by law. As such, there has been a call for the better use of resources to ensure that plant restoration and conservation are given a higher priority in biodiversity and land-management programs.

One flower that is not in any danger is the national flower, the thistle. The delicate purple blossom with sharp thorns is so tenacious that some people call it a weed. It has been a symbol of Scotland for nearly seven hundred years, and no one is quite sure how it came to that exalted honor. The flower has inspired legends and poetry, and is pictured on heraldic badges and other symbolic insignia. Interestingly, the thistle is also the logo of the *Encyclopædia Britannica,* which was first published in Edinburgh in 1768.

Purple thistle flowers bloom near a lake in Scotland.

Wind turbines turn in the hills and fields of Scotland.

ENERGY

Scotland aims to have 50 percent of all its energy consumption, including energy for transportation, come from renewable sources by 2030. In 2017, about 20 percent of its energy was from renewables.

Scotland is particularly well suited to achieving this goal. It has vast areas of water in its sea lochs and inland waters, and there have been major developments in exploiting the wave and tidal potential around the Scottish coast. There are several hydroelectric power stations in Scotland, and an energy converter has been installed off the island of Islay, which produces power for the National Grid. It is expected that the country will establish one of the few significant tide- and wave-energy markets in Europe in the coming years.

Electricity generation has made rapid progress toward a goal of 100 percent renewable sources by 2020. In 2015, Scotland generated 59 percent of its electricity consumption through renewable sources, and by 2018, that number had risen to 74 percent.

Scotland is the windiest country in Europe, and it is actively making use of it. In the last decade, it has built numerous onshore, or land-based, wind farms, and several offshore farms, with more planned. As of December 2018, it had a capacity of 7,800 megawatts (MW) from onshore wind generators and 623 MW of offshore sources. By 2019, the country's wind power was generating enough energy to power two Scotlands!

Nuclear power contributes about half of Scotland's electricity. However, the Scottish National Party (SNP) government—in power since 2007—has ceased building nuclear plants. Its "no new nuclear power strategy" is one that is at odds with the UK's policy of the expansion of nuclear energy. Only two nuclear plants continue to function in Scotland, but they are reaching the end of their lives.

INTERNET LINKS

https://www.environment.gov.scot
This site is a go-to resource for information on the Scottish environment.

https://www.sepa.org.uk/environment
The Scottish Environmental Protection Agency website has a wealth of facts about the country's environment.

THE SCOTS

A traditionally dressed Scotsman plays the bagpipes on a street in Edinburgh.

THOUGH SCOTLAND ACCOUNTS FOR 32 percent of the land area of the United Kingdom, the Scottish people make up a mere 8 percent of its population. They are a mix of the various ancient tribes that settled the country, along with a modern influx of people who migrated from other parts of Britain and abroad. The people of Scotland are properly called Scots, not Scotch. The term Scot has changed in meaning over the centuries. It originally referred to the Gaelic-speaking people of Ireland and Scotland. The Scottish kingdom became an amalgamation of the Celtic peoples, the Picts and the Gaels, with the Britons by the tenth century. Anglo-Saxon, Norse, French, and Anglo-Norman immigrants were eventually added to the mix.

Today, the population is around 5,440,000, and although the growth rate (0.2 percent) is slowing, the population continues to increase. Overall,

The word "clan" comes from the Gaelic *clan*, which means "children." Clans were named after a founder and had a rallying cry to bring warriors together in times of trouble. The Gaelic word for this cry, *sluagh-ghairm*, translates as "battle cry" and is the source of the English word "slogan."

the average age is increasing, as is the case in many other Western European countries. Life expectancy at birth is 77.1 years for males and 81.2 years for females, which is slightly lower than that of the UK in general, and roughly on par with the United States.

THE CELTS, PICTS, AND SCOTS

At the dawn of recorded history, Scotland was occupied by people who spoke different forms of Celtic languages. The Celtic languages are a branch of the Indo-European language family. The Celtic languages of Ireland, Britain, and Brittany (a region of France) are traditionally grouped into two main branches, Goidelic (Q-Celtic) and Brythonic (P-Celtic), because of a phonetic divergence that is thought to have developed in very ancient times.

By about the fifth century CE, there were three distinct ethnic and linguistic groups in Scotland: the Picts, a Celtic people closely related to the ancient Gauls; the Britons in the southwest, who spoke a language ancestral to modern Welsh; and the Dalriadic Gaels, or Scots, who were established along the western seaboard of Scotland.

The Dalriadic Scots are the real ancestors of Scottish culture and the Scottish nation. The term Scot originally referred to a Gaelic speaker, whether he was living in Scotland or Ireland. The kingdom of Scotland was built and dominated by Gaelic-speaking kings, saints, churchmen, and warriors, so the label stuck to Scotland rather than Ireland. At its height in the twelfth century, Gaelic was spoken in most parts of Scotland, and even south of the English border.

MODERN SCOTLAND

Over the centuries, the Picts and the Scots merged into one Gaelic-speaking community, but other groups have contributed to the ethnic diversity of the country. In the nineteenth century, many Irish arrived in Scotland, fleeing a terrible famine. Industrial development attracted workers from the north of England, and in the second half of the twentieth century, ethnic minorities from other parts of the world settled in Scotland.

According to the 2011 census, 84 percent of the respondents reported their ethnicity as "White: Scottish," and another 8 percent claimed "White: Other British." Other white ethnic groups made up another 8 percent, and minority ethnic groups made up 4 percent. That was an increase from 2 percent in the previous census of 2001.

Ethnic minorities in Scotland include Indians, Pakistanis, Bangladeshis, and Chinese, most of whom have migrated from other parts of Britain. Pakistanis make up the largest minority ethnic group, accounting for 1 percent of the Scottish population. Asian groups in general are the largest minority ethnic group, with 141,000 people making up 3 percent of the population. The African, Caribbean, or other black groups made up 1 percent of the population of Scotland in 2011, an increase of 28,000 people since 2001.

Another distinct cultural—if not ethnic—group in Scotland are the Gaelic speakers, who number about 59,000 people and live mostly in the Outer Hebrides. A larger number, 1.5 million, can speak Scots.

The next census is scheduled for 2021.

In this illustration from 1910, the legendary Fionn finds the old men of the forest.

SCOTTISH LEGENDS

Fionn mac Cumhaill (anglicized as Finn McCool) and his band of warriors, the Fianna (also known as the Fians or Feinne), were celebrated cultural heroes in Gaelic-speaking Scotland and Ireland throughout the Middle Ages and up to the present day. There are many songs and stories about Fionn and the Fianna and how they defended the Gaels from invaders such as the Vikings.

Robert (Rob Roy) MacGregor (1671—1734), a Highland chieftain and noted swordsman from the Trossachs, an area east and northeast of Loch Lomond, fought in the Jacobite Rising of 1715. His clan, the MacGregors, had been outlawed by the Scottish king in 1603 and survived on the social and economic margins of society until the ban against its name was lifted in 1774. Rob Roy was a hero in the fashion of Robin Hood among fellow Highlanders; there was

even a popular play about him performed in 1723. Many years after Rob Roy's death, his story was immortalized in English by Sir Walter Scott. He was glamorized even further in the 1995 Hollywood movie *Rob Roy*, which starred Liam Neeson.

Another Highlander who has passed into popular lore in English is Flora MacDonald (1722—1790), who sheltered Bonnie Prince Charlie—Prince Charles Edward Stewart—when he escaped the Hanoverians in his flight through Scotland. She dressed him as her maid Betty Burke when she might have claimed a reward of £30,000. Later, she emigrated to the present-day United States, where her family sided with the British during the American Revolution. Flora MacDonald returned to Scotland in 1778.

Scotland is a country steeped in history, and every locality has its own legends about the early Celtic saints who converted the local population, blessed local wells and healing sites, and performed miracles. Every clan has sagas about its founders; famous warriors and battles against rivals; and accomplished poets, musicians, and men of learning. No family was without many evenings' worth of tales and songs, which they sang and recited at parties called *ceilidhs* throughout the wintertime.

This statue of Flora MacDonald and her collie dog stands before Sheriff Court on Castle Hill in Inverness.

FAMOUS SCOTS

Scotland has produced many famous people in the fields of science and engineering. James Watt (1736—1819) modified the steam engine, and his improvements led to its being used widely. Watt also did a lot of research into electricity. John McAdam (1756—1836) gave his name to the material—tar macadam, or tarmac—that surfaces roads. Thomas Telford (1757—1834), a shepherd's son, was an engineer who built the Dean Bridge in Edinburgh, the Caledonian Canal linking the two coasts of Scotland, and the Göta Canal in Sweden. Charles Macintosh (1766—1843) invented several waterproof fabrics; James Young (1811—1883) was the first chemist to refine oil commercially; James Clerk Maxwell (1831—1879) proposed the notions of cybernetics and electromagnetism and created the world's first color photography process; and John Dunlop (1840—1921) invented the pneumatic tire.

Many other important inventors also hailed from Scotland. Sir James Dewar (1842—1923) created the vacuum flask; Alexander Graham Bell (1847—1922), a Scot who emigrated to the United States, invented the telephone; and Sir Alexander Fleming (1881—1955) discovered penicillin in 1928, although the drug took another eleven years to perfect. Other notable Scots who have given great contributions to the world include John Logie Baird (1888—1946), who invented an early form of television, and Marie Stopes (1880—1958), a pioneer in modern birth-control methods and founder of the world's first birth-control clinic. She was also an advocate of women's rights.

In 1996, the world was informed that Scottish embryologists had successfully cloned a sheep, Dolly, from the cells of an adult sheep.

This painting of James Dewar with the instruments of his laboratory is by Alfred Edmund Dyer.

THE CLANS AND TARTANS

Now a romantic shadow of its former self, the clan system once regulated Highland life. Highlanders gave or contracted their allegiances to chieftains, who led groups that acted as though they were extended families; in exchange, the supporters received the chieftain's protection. The chief could call on his clan members to fight in wars or work in the fields. In exchange, each member of the clan could expect to have his home, crops, and family well looked after and to receive counsel and support in times of need. As clans were semi-independent, they often vied with each other for power and territory. Clans were not strictly defined by ancestry; they were dynamic social organisms that expanded and shrank according to the effectiveness of their leaders, who could form contracts with the leaders of other smaller or larger groups.

Clans were originally distinguished in battle by wearing particular leaves of plants or trees in their bonnets: heather for the Donald clan, pine for the

MacGregors, and so on. Checkered cloth was made and worn across Scotland, but the particular technique of weaving the stripes of colors that we now know as tartan became associated with the Highlands in particular in the sixteenth century, when the belted plaid (or great kilt) was also developed by Scottish Gaels. Still, tartan was woven according to local designs and customs, not associated with specific clans. One purpose of wearing tartan cloth in the form of the belted plaid was to offer protection, warmth, and camouflage to travelers and Highland warriors, but bright colors were preferred by the wealthy to show off their ability to import expensive dyes.

After 1746, the wearing of tartan by males was restricted to the soldiers of British regiments. In the early nineteenth century, when Sir Walter Scott's novels romanticizing Highland life became popular, and King George IV was convinced to wear a kilt patterned in strong striped and checked colors, wearing tartans gained popularity. Clan tartans were formulated and manufactured to sell to a growing heritage industry in the nineteenth century, as people who had been removed from the land and traditional ways of life wanted to have symbols to remind them of their origins.

Today, the Scottish Register of Tartans is the country's official organization for registering and keeping track of tartan designs. Maintained and administered by the National Records of Scotland, its website features a searchable online database, including information on more than 2,700 patterns. These include clan and family tartans, royal tartans, state tartans from the United States, military tartans, and corporate tartans.

INTERNET LINKS

https://www.nrscotland.gov.uk
The National Records of Scotland has statistics, data, and information.

https://www.scotland.org/about-scotland/our-people
Various aspects of the Scottish people are presented on this site.

https://www.scotlandscensus.gov.uk
The Scottish census site includes a wealth of data. After 2021, it will report findings of the latest census.

LIFESTYLE

Scottish dancers wear traditional national costumes.

I N MANY WAYS, SCOTTISH LIFE IS MUCH like life in England or any Western European country. Most people live in urban environments, watch TV and movies, surf the internet, and enjoy sports. Young people hang out and listen to popular music; adults go to work and raise families; older folks reminisce about the way things were when they were young.

Despite being a part of the United Kingdom, though, Scotland maintains a vigorous sense of its own distinctive cultural life. National pride includes an embrace of those things that are most particularly Scottish—from whisky and traditional foods to country dancing, tartans and kilts, bagpipes, folk music, and Robert Burns.

The Scottish have a strong sense of egalitarianism. In recent years, they have prided themselves on being international leaders on topics such as human rights and climate change.

CITY LIFE

Life in the Scottish cities centers on thousands of pubs, designed in different styles to suit different customers. There are Victorian and Edwardian pubs for the older crowd, with quiet corners, peat fires, traditional music, lively games of darts, pub quizzes, and card games. For younger people, there are modern designer pubs, sports bars with huge screens showing soccer matches, and clubs, just as there are in England.

7

In general, Scotland has a healthy population. Comprehensive free health care for all is provided by the NHS (National Health Service) Scotland. Specialized services may require additional fees, but NHS Scotland always provides free accident and emergency treatment. For those who wish it, private care is also available through a private health insurance scheme. About 8.5 percent of people in Scotland have voluntary private health insurance.

Most people are away from home during the day, but families usually come together in the evening to share a meal. On weekday evenings, most families watch television, although people often incorporate a late evening visit to their local pub. Other social activities include going to the movies or the theater and playing bingo. On weekends, most people catch up with the business of running their homes, doing the shopping, taking children to social activities, attending church, and visiting their families.

Prior to the 1990s, shops kept very restricted hours and were closed for a half-day once a week. It is now possible to shop late in the evenings and on Sundays. Pubs also have longer opening hours.

Homes tend to be owned by individuals, although there are large areas of housing owned by the government. Row houses are common, with a tiny front yard and larger back garden. In older buildings, the toilet was located in the garden. Wealthier people own semidetached houses, which typically have three bedrooms, a small kitchen, two other downstairs rooms, a garden, and perhaps a garage. Apartment living has become very fashionable in cities, where old warehouses have been converted into modern open-plan apartments with shared leisure facilities such as a gym or a pool.

The number of single-person homes is on the increase in Scotland as elderly people are being left alone after the death of their spouse and younger people choose to live single lives. Two children are typical of the nuclear family; large families tend to be frowned on. The nuclear family is the typical unit, and grandparents usually live separately.

LIFE ON A CROFT

Most crofts are in the Highlands or on the Scottish islands. Until about World War II, the croft house was known as a *taigh tughaidh* (TIE too-ee), or thatched house. It was a one-story building with thick stone walls, about 6 feet (1.8 m) high. The corners of the house were rounded, and the roof was thatched and held down by ropes weighted with stones. Inside the single room were simple wooden furniture and an open hearth in the center, where the cooking was done. Fish-oil lamps were used to light up the house.

These houses have for the most part been replaced, but some still stand and are used as sheds or outhouses. Most modern crofts have solid-fuel stoves, electricity, and running water. They are also equipped with modern furniture and appliances such as refrigerators and washing machines.

Because of the isolation of the crofts, shopping or going to a movie means a long trip into town, either by car or by boat. Daily work consists of milking cows or tending sheep. Part of the day is spent farming salmon, fishing, or doing road work—whatever job the crofter has taken on to supplement his farm income.

EDUCATION

Scotland has its own education system that is separate from England and the rest of the UK. Most children start school at five years of age, although there are some state nursery schools that children attend from three years of age. Not all children are guaranteed a place in a state nursery, and priority is given to working mothers, often those employed by the state. The state nursery school system is supplemented by private nurseries and playgroups.

From ages five to twelve, children attend primary school, where they are taught according to a new state initiative called the Curriculum for Excellence. This program, launched in the 2012—2013 school year, aims to provide a wider, more flexible range of courses and subjects than was previously the norm. The Scottish government only sets guidelines about the school curriculum, and schools can make their own decisions on what to teach pupils. There are three core subjects that schools must teach—health and well-being, literacy, and mathematics.

In 2014, the Scottish government launched Learning for Sustainability, an educational initiative that aligns with the UN Sustainable Development Goals. In 2017, additional reforms gave more control over the curriculum to head teachers and parents. In 2019, the government launched Vision 2030, the final phase of the Learning for Sustainability Action Plan.

Secondary education lasts until age sixteen, at which point students take the national exams. Those who wish to qualify for further education can

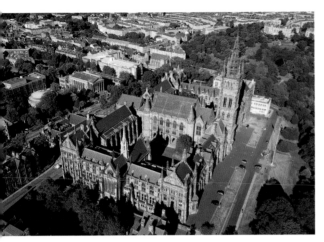

The University of Glasgow, as seen from above, is shown here.

continue for two more years of school in the Higher and Advanced Higher tracks, taking certifying exams for school graduation and entrance to university studies.

Both primary and secondary education are compulsory and provided free to children. After secondary school, education is by choice, but increasing numbers of students continue to study or take up vocational courses. Scotland has about 102 independent schools, of which 72 belong to the Scottish Council of Independent Schools (SCIS). Many are based on the English "public school" model (contrary to the name, these are actually private schools). In 2016, there were 29,647 pupils in SCIS independent schools, of which about 3,000 were in boarding school. Scotland's most famous boarding school, Gordonstoun School in Moray, is known for its emphasis on rugged outdoor experiences. It was attended by Prince Charles, the current heir to the British throne, and other members of the royal family.

Scotland has fifteen universities. The oldest are Saint Andrews, Glasgow, and Aberdeen—all founded in the fifteenth century—and Edinburgh, which was established in the sixteenth century. The newest is the University of the Highlands and Islands, which was granted university status in 2011. A degree from a Scottish university is different from an English or American degree. The program, which often lasts four years, awards the degree equivalent of a master of arts or science rather than bachelor's degree. In addition to the universities, there are further education colleges and higher education colleges—two different sorts of institutions—which grant diplomas similar to associate's or bachelor's degrees after two or more years of study.

LIFE'S BIG EVENTS

Life's big events—birth, coming-of-age, marriage, and death—have long been observed in the religion and customs of the Scottish people. However, participation in the ceremonies and traditions associated with these events has decreased in modern Scotland.

BIRTH   In the old days, Scotland treated children born out of wedlock differently than the rest of Britain did. In other parts of Britain, such a child was unable to inherit his or her father's estate, even if the parents subsequently married. In Scotland, however, marriage legitimized any children of the union. In the past, this brought about an unusual custom in the south of Scotland, called the hinding system. An agricultural worker was paid more if he brought his wife and children along to work, as he could produce more with the assistance of his family. This resulted in a situation where unmarried men hired young women in order to receive the maximum pay. The men often impregnated the women, and there was no stigma attached to such a pregnancy.

In modern times, questions of a child's "legitimacy" are no longer a concern. Women usually give birth in the local maternity hospital or with the help of a trained midwife if the family lives a long way from town. If the child's family follows traditional customs, there will be a christening, during which the child is formally accepted into the church and officially given his or her name. Godparents chosen by the parents promise to look after the spiritual well-being of the child. The child will be dressed for the occasion in an elaborate christening gown. After the ceremony, there is often a family party. At these events, it is customary to give the baby a gift made of silver.

Some ancient customs associated with childbirth are the groaning cheese and the groaning cake—special foods prepared for the mother during her confinement after childbirth. These are also given after the birth to young girls so that they have an easy delivery in the future. Another superstition is that the cradle and the baby buggy must be paid for in advance so that the unborn child will not grow up poor. However, these items must not be brought into the house before the baby's arrival. A very old Scottish practice was to plunge the newborn baby in cold water to make sure that it would start to breathe.

WEDDINGS   Marriages are less common in Scotland now than in previous times, but when a couple does get married, it is usually in a church. Weddings can also be performed in a registry office or at any other place of one's choice, as long as the ceremony is officiated by a minister. Gretna Green, located near the Scottish-English border, was for many years a place for runaway

Just as the United States has its own marriage capital in Las Vegas, there sits a town nestled on the border of Scotland and England called Gretna Green that is synonymous with clandestine marriages. In 1754, England passed a law that required all marriages to be recognized by a church and couples under twenty-one to have parental consent. At that time, Scotland was more liberal, and a marriage used to be considered legal so long as it was declared in front of two witnesses. Thus, it became a custom for young English couples who did not have parental consent to go to Scotland to get married. As Gretna Green is the first village over  *the Scottish border, many weddings were performed there. Due to the quirks of Scottish law, almost anyone could conduct the marriage ceremony. Most couples were married by the village blacksmith, but other residents also performed a fair share of the services.*

In 1857, Scottish law was changed to require twenty-one days' residence for marriage, and since 1929, both parties have to be at least sixteen years old to be married in Scotland, although no parental consent is needed. In 1977, however, the residential requirement was lifted, and Gretna Green remains a favored marriage location because of its romantic associations. The flourishing marriage industry boosts the economy of this small rural village, with hotels catering to families, pipers waiting to play wedding songs in the registry office, and many photographers taking pictures by the old blacksmith's forge.

English teens to marry because no parental consent was needed in Scotland. In England, anyone younger than eighteen who wishes to get married needs to prove the consent of his or her parents.

Weddings in Scotland are generally a big family affair. A service takes place in the family's place of worship and is followed by a reception at a local hotel for a large number of guests. Many people hire horse-drawn carriages or old-fashioned cars to get around. Traditionally, the bride wears a white dress and the groom wears a formal suit or a traditional outfit. The bride may be attended to by bridesmaids, and a best man helps the groom in his part of the ceremony.

DEATH   When a death occurs, even people who have little contact with the church will attend a service for the deceased. In Scotland, as in the rest of Britain, the tradition of keeping the deceased's body in the house for the wake is no longer practiced. Instead, a funeral director takes responsibility for the entire process: arranging the church service, the funeral paraphernalia, and the funeral procession.

Funerals are expensive, but they are not as elaborate as they were among wealthy Victorians, who built huge monuments to their dead. One surviving example of this is the Necropolis in Glasgow, where some 50,000 people were buried in some 3,500 tombs and many more graves of modest sizes. The tombs have been a major tourist attraction for more than one hundred years.

INTERNET LINKS

https://education.gov.scot
https://www.gov.scot/policies/schools
Both of these sites provide information about education in Scotland.

https://www.gretnagreen.com
Gretna Green has its own promotional site.

https://learningforsustainabilityscotland.org
RCE Scotland is the main site for the UN-aligned Learning for Sustainability initiative.

https://www.scotland.org/live-in-scotland/scottish-lifestyle
This Scotland tourism site takes a quick look at lifestyle.

https://scotland.shelter.org.uk/get_advice/advice_topics/finding_a_place_to_live/crofts_and_crofting
Crofts and crofting are explained in detail on this page.

RELIGION

The Free North Church of Scotland in Inverness in the Loch Ness Highlands is a typical Scottish church.

8

SCOTLAND IS A CHRISTIAN COUNTRY, historically and culturally. However, freedom of religion is enshrined in Scottish law.

The official church is the Church of Scotland, which claims 330,000 members and 800 ministers. Known as the Kirk, the church is legally recognized as the country's national church, but unlike the Church of England, which is the "established" church of England, it has no formal links with the state. The British monarch is the supreme governor of the Church of England, and the Archbishop of Canterbury is the most senior cleric. There are no equivalent leaders in the Church of Scotland. Indeed, the two Protestant churches are of two different denominations, with the Church of Scotland being Presbyterian and the Church of England being Anglican, or Episcopal. In Scotland, that sect is represented by the Scottish Episcopal Church.

The Methodist and Catholic Churches are also present in Scotland. There are Catholic congregations that survived the Reformation, especially in the Highlands, although descendants of Irish immigrants who arrived during the nineteenth century form the largest group of Catholics. In much smaller numbers are Jews, Muslims, Hindus, and Buddhists, all of whom practice their religions freely in Scottish cities. In Glasgow, there are many synagogues, mosques, and a Buddhist center.

Evidence of religion in Scotland dates back well before the arrival of Christianity and can be seen in the many standing stones and burial grounds of prehistoric times. Some aspects of these early religions, such as belief in fairies and other supernatural beings and powers, lingered in Scotland long after being officially outlawed by the church.

Candida Casa ("shining white house") at Whithorn, Galloway, founded around 400 CE by Saint Ninian, was the first Christian church in Scotland. Ninian was said to be the "apostle to the Southern Picts," but little is actually known about him. He is also known as Ringan and in Northern England as Trynnian. No historical person has yet been identified as Ninian, but some scholars believe he was likely Finnian of Movilla (ca. 495–589), an Irish Christian missionary.

THE EARLY CHRISTIANS

Christianity first came to Scotland in the time of the Romans. It made little impression on the inhabitants of Scotland until the sixth century CE, however, when Irish missionaries, led by Saint Columba, arrived and set up a monastery on Iona Island in the Inner Hebrides. This church led missions not only among the Gaels of the west of Scotland but also among the Picts in the north and east of Scotland, the Anglo-Saxons in England, and the peoples of the Continent. Iona and other centers of Christianity in Scotland were renowned seats of learning where literature was fostered and leadership advice was offered to the Gaelic-speaking kings of the Scots. The connections between religion and political power helped to unite the kingdom and spread the Gaelic language.

Gaelic monasteries were famous for the beautiful manuscripts they created, such as the Book of Kells, which was probably created on Iona Island. Like other aspects of Gaelic society, church positions and power tended to become concentrated in family dynasties. Clerics did not observe rules of celibacy, and many surnames, such as MacNab ("the son of the abbot") and MacTaggart ("the son of the priest"), reflect such family lineages.

Inchcolm Abbey on the island of Inchcolm in the Firth of Forth dates to the twelfth century.

Many monasteries such as Iona were in remote and isolated areas. Once the Vikings began to attack in the late eighth century, treasures were lost, and sites had to be abandoned. Gaelic church affairs and political interests were forced to move inland into the area of the Picts.

THE REFORMATION

The sixteenth century was the age of the European Reformation, a religious conflict between Protestants and Catholics. The Reformation, led by intellectuals such as Henry VIII, John Calvin, and Martin Luther, divided Western Europe for more than 150 years. Reformers broke away from the Roman Catholic Church and rewrote the Bible and church services in language that their congregations could understand, rather than learned languages such as Latin, Greek, and Hebrew, and removed hierarchy in churches.

In Lowland Scotland, Calvin's ideas took hold. A French philosopher who helped reform the church in Switzerland, Calvin advocated putting the Bible, rather than the word of the bishops, in the forefront of Christian religion. He believed in predestination—that if God is omniscient, or all-knowing, he must know what will happen to each and every person before they are born. This puts enormous pressure on the individual to behave in a godly manner to prove that he or she is one of the elect, the people predetermined by God to enter the kingdom of Heaven.

Led by John Knox, the Scottish reformers established their own church in 1560. However, the church was divided on whether to adopt the Presbyterian or Episcopalian form of government, the former preferring a church without state control and a hierarchy without bishops. More than a century of religious strife ended in 1689, when the Scottish Parliament and courts decreed that the Church of Scotland would be Presbyterian in government.

THE CHURCH OF SCOTLAND

The Church of Scotland is fiercely democratic and does not have a hierarchy or bishops. Laypeople as well as ministers run the Kirk, or church, and hold church courts to establish policy, but only ordained ministers can administer

Born in 1513 in Haddington in the Lothian region, John Knox was a Roman Catholic priest who was convinced by the Scottish reformer George Wishart to be part of the reformation of the Scottish church. After the archbishop of Saint Andrews burned Wishart for heresy, the reformers holed up in Saint Andrews Castle. In 1547, the governor of Scotland, with the help of the French, stormed the castle and arrested the reformers. Knox was sent to work on a ship as a slave. He was released nineteen months later through the intervention of the English. Knox returned to Scotland in 1559 and began to preach.

In 1560, the Church of Scotland was established. Schools were built in the Lowlands, and the church grew more powerful every year. John Knox died in 1572. There are memorials and statues erected to him all over Scotland. His influence even extends to the architecture of churches. Early churches that were elaborate Gothic creations gave way to simple buildings designed to enable the maximum number of people to listen to the preacher.

baptism and communion. Ministers, who can be either male or female, are chosen by the congregation, not appointed by a higher authority, and the leader of the Kirk, the moderator, assumes office for only a year. The churches are generally plain, with little decoration.

The doctrines of the church are moderate, but any kind of intellectual deviation is tolerated. In the nineteenth century, the Calvinist belief in predestination was moderated by theologians of the church who proposed that atonement was possible. Through good works and faith, anyone can go to heaven. Beliefs in the literal truth of the Bible were also challenged as scientists discovered that geology did not support the idea of a seven-day creation and Darwin's theories suggested that man had evolved, not been created.

Today, the Church of Scotland, similar to the Church of England, has adapted its ideas to suit scientific knowledge. A firmly held belief in the real existence of hell and the predetermined place of most human beings in it has given way to a belief that hell is not a physical place and that everyone can be redeemed.

The Gaelic name for Church of Scotland is Eaglais na h-Alba. In some of the churches, particularly in the Highlands and the Western Isles, there remain congregations that prefer Sunday services in Gaelic. This is also true of certain other Scottish denominations and even the Roman Catholic Church in the Outer Hebrides. In Edinburgh, Greyfriars Kirk of the Church of Scotland conducts services in both English and Scottish Gaelic, as does Saint Columba Church in Glasgow. However, finding ministers who can speak and preach in Gaelic has become difficult.

The Greyfriars Kirk in Edinburgh has long been an important church in the Scottish capital.

THE FREE CHURCH OF SCOTLAND

Early in the eighteenth century, the Church of Scotland split into two sects—the Moderates, who were concerned mainly with social matters and cultural activities, and the Evangelicals, who adhered strictly to Calvinist beliefs. In the nineteenth century, the Evangelicals wanted the church to be independent of the state and wanted the congregation, not the landowners who were patrons of the church, to choose its minister. When their demands were rejected, the Evangelicals decided to leave the church. At a general assembly of the Church of Scotland on May 18, 1843, two-fifths of the clergy walked out and formed a new church.

The Free Church of Scotland was very popular in the late nineteenth century. It enforced strict adherence to the rules regarding the Sabbath, or Sunday, and expected its members to attend services twice a day. In 1847, the Free Church joined the United Presbyterian Church, which had also broken away from the Church of Scotland. The main body of the Free Church reunited with the Church of Scotland in 1929 when the latter became independent of the state. Those who were against the union continued as the Free Church of Scotland.

The Free Church still dominates on the Outer Hebrides islands of Harris, North Uist, and Lewis. On the Sabbath, the islanders wear dark clothes and do no work, not even cooking. Any washing left over from the previous day must be brought inside, and fishing boats must be at anchor. Until recently, few ferries ran to the islands on Sundays.

ROMAN CATHOLICISM

Roman Catholicism was the pre-Reformation religion of Scotland. In the eighteenth century, about twenty thousand people—chiefly in remote rural areas—were still Roman Catholic, but vigorous missionary activity promoting Protestantism, especially in the Highlands, brought about dramatic changes in the religious complexion of the region.

The mix of religions, especially in the Lowlands, changed again in the nineteenth century with the influx of refugees from Ireland to Scottish cities. By 1951, there were about 750,000 Roman Catholics in Scotland, mainly of Irish descent. Catholicism is strongest in urban areas where the Irish first settled, but there is also a strong tradition of Catholicism in Aberdeenshire, in the eastern Highlands, and among the southern Hebrides, on the islands of South Uist, Eriskay, and Barra.

OTHER RELIGIONS

Scotland has many other religious groups—either sects of Christianity or other religions. The Episcopal Church is strong among the upper classes of Scotland. It is the equivalent of the Church of England and observes more-ornate rituals than the Presbyterian churches do. The Free Presbyterian Church, a radical sect that still flourishes in Scotland, believes the pope to be the Antichrist and Roman Catholic mass to be a blasphemy. There are also Baptist churches and several Evangelical groups, as well as communities of Jews, Hindus, and Muslims.

RELIGION TODAY

Following a trend that is evident across much of Europe, religion is in decline in Scotland. The Kirk and other churches report declining numbers, as fewer Scottish people report being religious. The 2011 census asked people to report their religious affiliation, and the results largely verified that trend: 37 percent said "no religion" (compared with 27 percent in 2001); 32 percent answered "Church of Scotland" (compared with 42 percent in 2001); 16 percent said "Roman Catholic" (no change since 2001); 1.4 percent said "Islam" (compared with 0.8 percent in 2001); and around 0.1 percent each answered "Buddhism," "Sikhism," "Judaism," and "Hinduism."

The results of the 2021 census will be telling. Until then, however, a more recent poll in 2017, conducted by the Humanist Society of Scotland, found 23.6 percent of Scottish respondents said they were religious, while 72.4 percent said they were not. However, some critics of the poll argue that the question "Are you religious?" is not easily answered with a simple "yes" or "no" and does not allow for the many levels of human spiritual experience.

INTERNET LINKS

https://www.bbc.co.uk/religion/religions/christianity/subdivisions/churchofscotland_1.shtml
This report is a profile of the Church of Scotland and related denominations.

https://www.churchofscotland.org.uk
The official site of the Church of Scotland presents up-to-date information.

https://www.undiscoveredscotland.co.uk/usscotfax/society/religion.html
This is a quick overview of religion in Scotland historically and today.

LANGUAGE

Welcome to Scotland

Fàilte gu Alba

A Scottish border sign extends a
welcome in English and Gaelic.

9

S COTLAND HAS THREE OFFICIALLY recognized languages: English, Scots, and Gaelic. The dominant language of Scotland is English, but that is a relatively recent development. The early inhabitants, the Picts, spoke a Celtic language that was closely related to ancient Gaulish. Several words that can still be found in place names in Scotland, such as *pit* and *aber*, come from Pictish.

Another language spoken in southern Scotland by an early tribe, the Britons, was Brythonic, the ancestor of modern Welsh. The word *caer*, meaning "fort," which appears in some place names, is a remnant of that language.

In the ninth century CE, another language entered the melting pot—the Norse language (later known as Norn), spoken by the Viking settlers of the Orkney and Shetland Islands. In parts of Shetland, Norn was spoken until the eighteenth century. The influence of Norn can still be seen in place names that contain the words *bister*, meaning "farmstead;" *by*, or "village;" and *wick*, meaning "bay."

GAELIC

Gaelic, a Celtic language, was probably first brought to Scotland from Ireland in the fourth and fifth centuries CE. It took hold in the area of

In 2018, the top baby names in Scotland were Jack and Olivia. Jack had been the top boys' name for eleven years running. It was followed by Oliver, James, Logan, and Lewis. By 2018, Olivia had maintained its top spot as the most popular girls' name for three years, followed by Emily, Isla, Sophie, and Amanda.

Argyll on the Scottish west coast. By the tenth century, Gaelic had become the native tongue in most of Scotland, supplanting the earlier Pictish, which died out. More place names in Scotland are Gaelic than any other language.

Over time, the language developed differently from the Gaelic tongue in Ireland. In Ireland, Gaelic is called Irish, or the Irish language. In Scotland, however, it is called Scottish Gaelic, or simply Gaelic. (In addition to those two Celtic tongues, there are four other Celtic languages that survive, or barely survive, today—Cornish, which went extinct a couple of centuries ago in southwest Britain, but which was revived in the twentieth century; Welsh, spoken in Wales; Manx, spoken on the Isle of Man; and Breton, which is spoken in Brittany, in northwestern France.)

Gaelic was associated with a highly developed law system, literature, and a prestigious culture. An elegy written to Saint Columba on his death in 597 is the oldest surviving poem in the Gaelic language, giving Gaelic literature a pedigree as old as any other in Western Europe. Poets held important status in Gaelic society. They served wealthy patrons who depended on them as public-relations servants, composing songs to praise them and satirize their enemies. A fully qualified professional poet spent about seven years studying grammar, linguistics, and history; he memorized examples of the more than three hundred poetic meters and composed poems on subjects assigned by his teacher.

Many highly sophisticated Gaelic poems remain from the medieval period that praise or satirize the MacDonalds, the Campbells, the MacLeans, and other great clans and chieftains of the Highlands. Gaelic songs and poems composed in the seventeenth century and even earlier continue to be sung by people today because of their beauty and powerful evocation of people and events.

After the thirteenth century, as the influence of the English and the French spread across the Lowlands and wealth and land systematically began to be transferred into the hands of people who spoke a form of Middle English, Gaelic began to be replaced by the language of the Normans in the Lowlands. As trade increased, Anglophone and Flemish merchants settled in the towns, providing another incentive to speak English.

The Jacobite Risings and the Highland Clearances in the eighteenth and nineteenth centuries accelerated the decline of Gaelic. In 1872, the Education Act required all children to attend Scottish schools but made English the de facto language. Children were punished for speaking Gaelic in the classroom. In Scotland, about 87,000 people report being able to speak some Gaelic, but only 57,375 people speak it fluently. They are mostly in the northwestern Highlands and the Hebrides.

In recent decades, there has been an increase in interest in preserving and reclaiming the language. Gaelic is now taught in school, though it isn't mandatory as it is in Ireland. There are now some bilingual primary schools, and on the Isle of Skye there is even a Gaelic college, Sabhal Mòr Ostaig. In addition, there has been an enormous increase in the number of Gaelic-language television and radio programs, and publishing in Gaelic is flourishing.

Gaelic made its way to North America by way of immigrants from the mid-eighteenth century to the early twentieth century. Today, it survives in this region only in Nova Scotia, Canada.

Cards to help children learn Gaelic hang in a Scottish primary school classroom.

SCOTS

Scots, or Lallans, used to be widely spoken in southern and eastern Scotland, but there is concern that the number of people who speak it and the richness of its vocabulary are in decline. Scots—which was referred to as "Inglis" into the sixteenth century—comes from Northern English, which gradually replaced Gaelic as the lingua franca (common language) in the royal court and the Lowlands beginning in the eleventh century. By 1424, Scots had replaced Latin as the official language of government. In the fourteenth to sixteenth centuries, a literary Scots language developed.

Scots and Northern English drifted apart in the fifteenth and sixteenth centuries. In the mid-1500s, however, the language of the Scots became more anglicized as the power of England increased. During the Reformation, English was used as the language of the Bible. By the eighteenth century, Scots was regarded as the language of the common people.

Today, Scots is considered a regional dialect, though some linguists see it as its own language with its own dialects. In any event, it's listed as "vulnerable" by UNESCO. In the 2011 census, about 1.5 million people identified themselves as Scots speakers. Scots is used only in Scotland; it is not spoken anywhere else in the world. There is no standard spoken or written form of the language.

The Robert Burns Birthplace Museum is in Alloway, South Ayrshire.

"To a Mouse, on Turning Her Up in Her Nest with the Plough" is one of Robert Burns's most beloved poems. Also known as "To a Mouse," the 1785 poem is about accidently overturning a mouse's nest with a plow.

At right is a UK postage stamp honoring the "wee beastie."

To demonstrate the difference in Burns's Scots and today's English, here is an excerpt, with translation.

SCOTS

Wee, sleekit, cow'rin, tim'rous beastie,
O, what a panic's in thy breastie!
Thou need na start awa sae hasty
Wi bickering brattle!
I wad be laith to rin an' chase thee,
Wi' murd'ring pattle!

ENGLISH

Small, crafty, cowering, timorous little beast,
Oh, what a panic is in your breast!
You need not start away so hasty
With your hurrying scamper!
I would be loath to run and chase you,
With murdering plough-staff!

The grammar of Scots is very similar to that of English, but the spelling and vocabulary are different. Many Scots words do not exist in the English language. Examples of these are *dreich* (DREECH), meaning "dull;" *daundring* (DORN-dring), or "walking slowly;" and *roup* (ROOP), meaning "auction." In addition, Scots retains some words that were once part of the English language but have since disappeared. For instance, in Scots the plural of "shoe" is *shuin*, and the plural of "eye" is *een*.

The most famous writer in the Scots language is the poet Robert Burns (1759—1796), who collected old folk songs and rewrote them in his own style. A modern writer who used Scots was the poet Hugh MacDiarmid (1892—1978).

Here are some words in Scots, English, and Gaelic:

SCOTS	ENGLISH	SCOTTISH GAELIC
auld	*old*	seann
bairn	*baby*	pàisde
bonnie	*pretty*	breagha
daft	*stupid*	gòrach
fey	*under the influence of the fairies*	litreachadh
frae	*from*	bho
gab	*the mouth, or talking too much.*	bruidhinn cus
ken	*understand*	tuigsinn
laird	*landowner*	uachdaran
lug	*ear*	cluais
mair	*more*	tuilleadh
muckle	*a lot of*	gu leòr
sassenach	*foreigner*	cèin
wean	*child*	leanabh
wee	*small*	beag

* One language is never enough!

SCOTTISH ENGLISH

Any English-speaking person who visits Scotland will have no difficulty in understanding what is said after the initial difficulties of accents and usage are overcome. In most parts of Britain, a linguistic phenomenon called the Great Vowel Shift took place during medieval times. Anyone who has read Geoffrey Chaucer's works will recognize that the English language has changed enormously over the centuries. Chaucer's English predates the vowel shift and is closer to the English spoken in some parts of Scotland, where the shift did not occur. Thus, you might hear a Scot saying *tak* instead of the English "take," or *bool* instead of the English "bowl."

In addition, English usage in Scotland has changed or been influenced by Scots or Gaelic over the years. For example, when English people say, "I doubt you'll need an umbrella," they mean that it is not going to rain. However, when Scottish people say the same words, they mean that it *will* rain! They use the expression "I doubt that" to mean "I'm sorry to say that." Likewise, to an Englishman, "doing the messages" means sending email to people; to a Scot, it means shopping for groceries. To a Scot, "I'll see you the length of the bus stop" means the speaker will walk you to the bus stop; to the English, it means nothing at all.

September 2019 newspaper front pages in Scotland are shown here.

INTERNET LINKS

https://www.gov.scot/publications/scots-language-policy-english
The Scottish government site details its commitment to preserving the Scots language.

https://www.omniglot.com/writing/gaelic.htm
Omniglot offers information and videos about Gaelic.

https://www.omniglot.com/writing/scots.htm
This language site provides a good introduction to Scots.

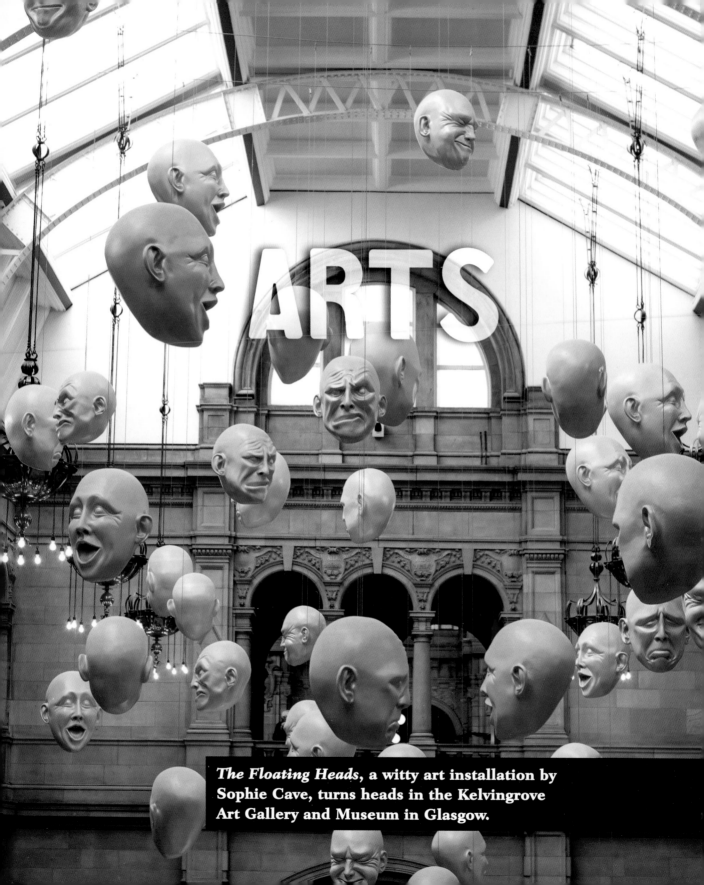

ARTS

The Floating Heads, a witty art installation by Sophie Cave, turns heads in the Kelvingrove Art Gallery and Museum in Glasgow.

10

THERE MUST BE SOMETHING IN THE water, because Scottish creativity flows like the falls of Eas a' Chual Aluinn (the highest waterfall in the United Kingdom). Besides producing more than its share of the world's scientists and inventors, Scotland has contributed to the world's culture in no small measure. Scottish music, which has a long tradition, flourishes today, either in its original form or as contemporary music.

Famous Scottish writers include Sir Walter Scott, Robert Burns, and John Buchan. Scotsman J. M. Barrie is best known for writing *Peter Pan*. Born in Edinburgh, writer Arthur Conan Doyle gave the world Sherlock Holmes. The prolific writer Alexander McCall Smith continues to delight readers worldwide. Also, J. K. Rowling, author of the *Harry Potter* books is not really Scottish, but she lives there. Indeed, she has lived most of her adult life in Scotland, and she wrote *Harry Potter* there as well!

No list of Scottish writers would leave out Robert Louis Stevenson. The Scottish novelist and travel writer produced some of the most beloved stories in the English language—*Treasure Island*, *Kidnapped*, *Strange Case of Dr. Jekyll and Mr. Hyde*, and *A Child's Garden of Verses,* along with many poems, short stories, and nonfiction travel articles.

In 2004, the Scottish Parliament created the position of the Scots Makar. The position's name comes from an old Scottish word, *makar*, for poet or bard. The first recipient was Edwin Morgan, considered one of the foremost Scottish poets of the twentieth century, followed in 2011 by Liz Lochhead and in 2016 by the renowned poet Jackie Kay.

SHETLAND MUSIC

The Shetland Islands have a long tradition of fiddle playing in a distinctive style. Like numerous other Scottish traditions, this style of music came very close to extinction in the 1970s, when young people on the islands migrated to the cities in search of better work opportunities, and the music was not passed along to the next generation. However, Shetland music, as well as other types of Scottish music, has undergone a revival in recent times, thanks to performers who tirelessly promote it.

The most famous proponent of Shetland music is Aly Bain, who is also a novelist and a television presenter. Together with other musicians from Ireland and Scotland, he formed a band called Boys of the Lough, which enjoyed success for twenty-five years. This band encouraged young Shetlanders to take up the fiddle. In the twenty-first century, Shetland music has a strong and vibrant future.

TRADITIONAL MUSIC

Scotland has a proud musical tradition, one that is interwoven with its history and culture. Although Scottish music has influenced and been influenced by Irish traditional music, it is very much a creature unto itself, and while many other traditional forms of music have lost popularity to pop music, traditional Scottish music remains a vital and living force.

Perhaps the most ancient form of traditional Scottish music is Gaelic folk music, and it continues to thrive, not just in the Highlands but also across the rest of the country. Characteristic of Gaelic music is harp playing, which has been revived in recent years by contemporary musicians. The piping tradition is also strongly connected to Gaelic singing, as is the fiddle, which appeared in Scotland in the seventeenth century.

Like many other countries, Scotland underwent a roots revival in the 1960s. During this time, folk songs and traditional music began to engage young Scots who felt separated from their country's culture. Folk singing was revived by artists such as Ewan MacColl and Jean Redpath, who was best known for recording the songs of Robert Burns, and by groups such as the Gaugers.

Scottish Celtic bands include Capercaillie, Runrig, Breabach, and many others. Folk and Celtic-fusion musicians include singer-songwriter Dougie MacLean; singer, harpist, and fiddler Rachel Newton; and singer-songwriter Claire Hastings. Julie Fowlis, born in 1978 in the Outer Hebrides, sings mostly in Scottish Gaelic. Along with her many albums, she is known for singing the theme song to the animated film *Brave*, which takes place in Scotland.

THE BAGPIPES Although the bagpipes are strongly associated with Scotland today, they are not exclusively a Scottish instrument. They were said to have originated in the Near East, and there are versions of the pipes throughout Europe and even in India and Russia. Bagpipes are thought to have appeared in Scotland in the fifteenth century. Although today in Scotland there are two dominant types of bagpipes—bellows (or "small") pipes, which create sound using a bellows held under the piper's arm, and the great Highland bagpipe, which is blown using the mouth—a wider variety existed in the eighteenth and nineteenth centuries.

Julie Fowlis and her band perform at Folkfest in Killarney, Ireland.

The great Highland bagpipe is the type most commonly played today. It consists of a bag that is inflated by blowing into a leather blowpipe. The bag is held under one arm. By squeezing the bag, the player can control the amount of air that flows through the other pipes—three drones and a chanter—which have double reeds. The piper plays songs on the chanter, which has eight finger holes.

The great Highland bagpipe produces a very large sound that can be heard at a long distance, so it is no wonder that it was used to summon people, wake them up, and give signals for battle. The bellows pipes, which are softer, are well suited to indoor activities, such as dances.

Although any kind of song can be adapted for the nine-note scale of the bagpipes, songs in the Highland musical tradition have generally been categorized as *ceòl beag* (cowal BEG), which literally means "small music" and often refers to dance music, or *ceòl mór* (cowal MOR), literally "big music," a classical tradition requiring effort and concentration for both the player and listener. Ceòl mór is usually referred to as pibroch in English; it consists of a basic theme, the *ùrlar* (oor-LAWR), and a number of increasingly complex variations.

THE ACCORDION   The accordion has long been a part of Scottish music. In the early twentieth century, the melodeon, which is a type of accordion, was popular among rural folk. It was popularized by Jimmy Shand, a musician who played Scottish dance music. By expanding and squeezing the bellows, the accordionist forces air over the sets of free reeds inside the instrument, causing the reeds to vibrate and make sounds.

THE FIDDLE   The fiddle is the mainstay of most Scottish music. It may have first come to Scotland with the crusaders. The fiddle works the same way as a violin, but it is used in traditional music. Fiddle songs have been written about historical people and events, the supernatural, and even disasters. Some very good fiddle songs came out of the Jacobite period. Legendary fiddlers include William Marshall and Niel Gow. Scottish fiddling is the root of much American folk music, such as Appalachian fiddling, and it is largely seen in Cape Breton, Nova Scotia, an island on the east coast of Canada.

THE HARP   The harp has a long, ancient history in Scotland. Most Celtic harps are small and can be played on the knee. The Scottish harp is called a *clarsach*. Until the end of the Middle Ages, the clarsach was the most popular musical instrument in Scotland, and harpists were among the most prestigious cultural figures in the courts of Scottish chieftains, kings, and earls. Harpists enjoyed special rights and played a crucial part in ceremonial occasions such as coronations. Most modern players use nylon or gut strings, but some have gone back to the original wire-strung harp, with its bell-like sound.

Harpist Fiona Hyslop gives a performance during the Edinburgh International Harp Festival at Merchiston Castle.

SCOTTISH MUSIC TODAY

Many traditional music bands continue to perform today. In addition, Scotland has produced a number of rock bands, but it was only during the post-punk era of the early 1980s that the country really came into its own with bands such as the Associates, Eurythmics (featuring Annie Lennox), and Simple Minds. Since then, Scotland has produced a steady stream of rock acts. The 1980s also saw the rise of Scottish progressive rock and metal.

The late 1990s and the 2000s have produced a number of Scottish guitar bands, which have gone on to achieve critical or commercial success. These bands include Franz Ferdinand, Travis, the Fratellis, and Belle and Sebastian.

Scottish piping has become popular again in recent times. Pipers such as Gordon Duncan and Fred Morrison began to explore new musical genres on different types of pipes. Traditional music and dance have also had a revival, sustained by dedicated groups and associations, major nationwide competitions, and a tradition of informal music-making in pubs. The popularity of the *ceilidh*, a public event of traditional dances set to fiddle songs, has also contributed to the revival of traditional music.

POETS

Probably the most beloved Gaelic poet is Donnchadh Bàn Mac an t-Saoir, called Duncan Ban MacIntyre in English. He was born in Glen Orchy in 1724 and worked as a gamekeeper in the Highlands during a time of great social and environmental change. One of his most celebrated poems is in praise of the mountain Ben Doran; it describes the plants and animals that lived on the mountain and the hunting of deer. Despite being conscripted into the Hanoverian forces during the Jacobite Rising of 1745, he composed a song in praise of Prince Charles and another song complaining that civilian men were not allowed to wear tartans and kilts in 1746. In 1767, he moved to Edinburgh and took a job with the City Guard until 1806.

Another important—and more recent—Gaelic poet was Somhairle MacGilleain, a.k.a. Sorley MacLean (1911—1996). His work was a fusion of

Robert Burns (1759–1796), the national poet of Scotland, is as famously Scottish as tartans, bagpipes, and haggis. Born in Alloway in the southwest of the country, he wrote in his native language, Lowland Scots. Best known the world round for his song "Auld Lang Syne," which has become a New Year's Eve anthem, he is also beloved for such works as "Tam o' Shanter," "A Red, Red Rose," "To a Mouse," and "Address to a Haggis." His work sentimentalizes ordinary people and satirizes the church and the state.

Burns was born to a large family. His father, a tenant farmer, died in debt. As such, the young poet resented politicians and rich landlords. When Burns became head of the family, he found a farm to live on. In his free time, he wrote poetry for his own amusement and to entertain his friends. Similar to his father, Burns did not have much success as a tenant farmer and wanted to leave Scotland. Before he did, he published his poetry. Poems, Chiefly in the Scottish Dialect *(1786) became popular and was enjoyed by both the intellectuals in Edinburgh and ordinary people. Burns moved to Edinburgh, but he left after a while because he was unhappy there.*

He later found a job collecting and rewriting traditional Scottish ballads, producing songs such as "Auld Lang Syne," "Comin' Through the Rye," and "Green Grow the Rashes." Burns never received any payment for his work, as he saw what he was doing as a way of contributing to his country. He died in Dumfries at age thirty-seven of rheumatic heart disease.

Robert Burns's birthday, January 25—"Robbie Burns Day"—is celebrated in Scotland as well as by fans living overseas with "Burns Suppers," which feature readings, music, and of course, haggis.

traditional and modern elements. He has been credited with "saving Scottish Gaelic poetry" and reinvigorating and modernizing the Gaelic language. His melancholy poem "Hallaig," published in 1954, is arguably his most popular work. The poem, about a deserted town in the Hebrides Islands, abandoned during the Highland Clearances, was translated into English in 2002 by the great Irish poet Seamus Heaney.

THE MOVIE INDUSTRY

In 2018, there were four hundred film and video companies in Scotland, employing about 3,635 people. In addition, there are numerous foreign films about or filmed in Scotland.

Two films seem to sum up the different faces of Scotland. *Braveheart* (1995), an American movie about Scottish warrior William Wallace, conjures up a romantic image of a strong but downtrodden nation fighting for its soul and independence. In *Trainspotting* (1996), a British film starring Scottish actors Ewan McGregor, Ewen Bremner, Kevin McKidd, Robert Carlyle, and Kelly Macdonald, drug addicts eke out a degraded existence. One of them berates Scotland for being conquered by the English.

More recently, the 2019 American movie *Robert the Bruce*, starring Scottish actor Angus Macfadyen, opened at the Edinburgh Film Festival to mixed reviews. Meanwhile, Scotland has also captured audiences' imaginations through the fantasy time-travel TV series *Outlander*. Starring Scottish actor Sam Heughan and featuring fellow Scotsmen like Graham McTavish and Gary Lewis, much of the action of the show takes place in the Scottish Highlands during the time of the Jacobite Risings. The series, which began in 2014, was filmed largely on location in Scotland.

In addition to the actors mentioned above, some other Scottish actors who have achieved international recognition include Sean Connery of *James Bond* fame and other films; Robbie Coltrane, best known for protraying Rubeus Hagrid in the *Harry Potter* film series; Karen Gillan, known for playing Nebula in the *Guardians of the Galaxy* and *Avengers* films, and David Tennant of *Doctor Who*.

"Poetry, the reading of it, the writing of it, the saying it out loud, the learning of it by heart, matters deeply to ordinary Scottish people everywhere."

–Liz Lochhead, poet, dramatist, and Scots Makar from 2011 to 2016

Glamis Castle is an impressive sight on a sunny day in Angus, Scotland.

ARCHITECTURE

The earliest known examples of Scottish architecture are at Skara Brae on Orkney, a cluster of ten houses built in stone between 3180 BCE and 2500 BCE. As Europe's most complete Neolithic village, it has gained UNESCO World Heritage status.

The brochs, round stone structures built on the coastal areas of Scotland during the Iron Age, are also stunning architectural achievements. These large stone towers were shaped so intelligently and built so sturdily that some still stand two thousand years after they were built.

The typical Scottish castle is in fact a fortified tower house built for defense as well as accommodation. The defensive nature shows in the bare ground floor; windows and decoration appear only above ground level so that attackers do not have easy access. After the seventeenth century, more and more living quarters were added, until the tower houses began to resemble fairy-tale

In terms of painting, one of the most famous works by a Scottish artist is The Reverend Robert Walker Skating on Duddingston Loch, *better known as* The Skating Minister. *The image is beloved well beyond Scotland and is considered almost as Scottish as tartans and bagpipes.*

The man on the skates was an actual person, a Church of Scotland minister born in 1755. He was a member of the Edinburgh Skating Club, which is said to be the world's first figure skating club. The artist is somewhat less certain than the subject. The painting is attributed to Henry Raeburn (1756–1823), a Scottish portrait painter based in Edinburgh. However, in 2005, the Scottish National Portrait Gallery caused quite a hubbub by suggesting the iconic painting might actually have been made by a French artist, Henri-Pierre Danloux. Raeburn fans were flummoxed and furious. Though there is no firm evidence to support either artist, eventually art historians at the gallery were convinced that Raeburn probably did, in fact, paint the graceful, gliding clergyman.

Today, the painting hangs in the National Gallery in Edinburgh.

castles, which the Scottish tourist board now uses in advertisements. Glamis Castle in Angus, which dates mostly to the seventeenth century, is a typical castle of this sort, with plenty of ornamental turrets and other embellishments on the top floors but plain walls with no windows below.

Castles built in the eighteenth and even nineteenth century had all the grand scale of older castles, but the defensive element of their design was gone. Big ground-floor windows, huge entrance staircases, massive doors, and many entrances were typical design features.

For cutting-edge modern architecture, however, Scotland's first design museum, the V&A Dundee, is about as state-of-the-art as art can get. Opened in 2018, this dramatic museum in Dundee is an extension of London's famed Victoria and Albert Museum. The building was designed by Japanese architect Kengo Kuma, who said his design was inspired by the cliffs on the east coast of Scotland. Inside, the Scottish Design Galleries feature permanent design works from across Scotland, along with changing exhibitions about design in fashion, video games, robots, and many other subjects yet to come.

SCOTTISH ARTISTS

The man who bridged the gap between art and architecture in the modern age was Charles Rennie Mackintosh (1868—1928). As a child, he painted the countryside where he lived, and as a teenager he attended the Glasgow School of Art. His design ideas fused art nouveau with influences from Japanese art and the artist Aubrey Beardsley. In 1896, Mackintosh won the competition to design the new Glasgow School of Art building, which is considered his greatest work. He also designed interiors of buildings, and it is for his designs for crockery, interior decoration, and furniture that Mackintosh is most famous. He retired to Suffolk and later to France, where he concentrated on drawing. Mackintosh was dismissed as an eccentric in Scotland, but his work gained recognition in the rest of Europe. It is only in the past forty or so years that his talent has been acknowledged in Scotland.

In the 1880s, a group of young men studying at the Edinburgh Royal Scottish Academy became known as the Glasgow Boys. They were strongly influenced by the French impressionists and painted rural scenes as well as scenes of street life in the city. They rejected the traditional Scottish style of historical and allegorical scenes painted in a romantic fashion as unreal and sentimental. The chief proponents of the Glasgow Boys' style were Sir James Guthrie, Sir John Lavery, George Henry, and E. A. Hornel. The Glasgow Boys had a major effect on Scottish art, altering it forever and giving it a new life.

INTERNET LINKS

https://www.clairehastings.com
Claire Hastings's home site has audio tracks and videos.

https://www.economist.com/prospero/2019/01/23/why-scottish -folk-music-is-thriving
This article examines the recent revival of interest in traditional music among a new generation.

https://www.nationalgalleries.org/art-and-artists/5327/reverend -robert-walker-1755-1808-skating-duddingston-loch
The Scottish National Galleries site offers an engaging discussion about *The Skating Minister*.

https://www.nytimes.com/2014/08/24/arts/music/jean-redpath -prolific-scottish-folk-singer-dies-at-77.html
The *New York Times* reviews the life and extraordinary contribution of the folk singer Jean Redpath.

https://www.poetryfoundation.org/poets/robert-burns
This poetry site takes an in-depth look at Robert Burns and his life and times.

http://www.sorleymaclean.org/english
The poet Sorley MacLean is lauded here.

https://www.theguardian.com/books/2002/nov/30/ featuresreviews.guardianreview35
An English translation of "Hallaig" by Sorley MacLean can be found on this page.

https://www.vam.ac.uk/dundee
This is the site of the V&A Dundee design museum.

LEISURE

Helmeted players compete in a shinty-hurling match between Scotland and Ireland. This hybrid game merges the rules of Scottish shinty and Irish hurling.

THE SCOTS ENJOY A WIDE RANGE OF activities in their leisure time, from traditional Scottish Highland games to the British national game of soccer. Other popular sports include shinty, skiing, and fishing. Golf was invented in Scotland.

Scotland hosts many of its own sporting competitions, and it enjoys independent representation at several international sporting events. Scotland's national sport is soccer, a game that has been played in the country since the fifteenth century.

For the less active, watching television, going to the movies, and playing or listening to music are the preferred leisure activities. The cities have casinos, theaters, movie theaters, concert halls, and art galleries to occupy a Scot's leisure time. Many people have gardens, and gardening became a big-business leisure industry during the past decade, with people spending as much on plants and garden furnishings as they do on decorating the interior of their homes.

SHINTY

Scotland's oldest known game is shinty, called *camanachd* (KAH-min-auk) in Gaelic. It can be traced back to the Iron Age and was played by Celtic peoples across the British Isles. Different forms of shinty were played in Scotland and elsewhere and were brought to North America by immigrants. It is one of the inspirations of the modern game of hockey. Shinty was traditionally played by teams of boys on New Year's Day.

Getting out into the natural world is enormously popular in Scotland. Mountain biking, hiking, hillwalking (which is exactly what it sounds like—a form of hill or low mountain climbing without need of special equipment), kayaking, or just relaxing by a loch are wonderful outdoorsy activities.

In the old days, clans in the Highlands would compete against each other in sporting events and tests of strength. The Highland Games only took their modern form in the nineteenth century, when Queen Victoria took an interest in Scottish culture and Highlanders were idealized as loyal soldiers. Today, the games take place throughout summer at events that resemble festivals, complete with plenty of colorful fanfare.

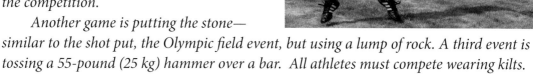

Tossing the caber (shown at right) is the most spectacular of the games. A strong man lifts an entire tree trunk with its branches removed—a caber—and runs a required distance with it. At the end of the run, he must throw the caber. The distance the caber travels, grace in running, and accuracy of throw determine the winner of the competition.

Another game is putting the stone— similar to the shot put, the Olympic field event, but using a lump of rock. A third event is tossing a 55-pound (25 kg) hammer over a bar. All athletes must compete wearing kilts.

Tourism has altered the Highland Games a bit. They are now geared to visitors and include parachute jumps, celebrity appearances, fairs, and exhibitions of dancing and piping.

FOOTBALL

Soccer (called football outside of the United States) is a worldwide phenomenon in which Scotland participates enthusiastically. Every Saturday during fall and winter and throughout spring, thousands of supporters stream to soccer grounds to stand in often cold, damp, and uncomfortable conditions to watch their teams play. Soccer support is tribal in nature, and fans spend the entire match singing songs about the superb qualities of their own team, the inadequacies of the opposing team, and the questionable calls by the referee. At big matches where a lot depends on the outcome, there is occasional violence between supporters of the two teams.

At the local level, there is the Scottish Football League, which has three divisions. The best clubs play in the Scottish Premier League, which is dominated by two teams, Celtic and Rangers. Based in Glasgow, these teams do not represent areas in Glasgow but religious groups; Celtic is the Catholic team, and Rangers the Protestant. When these two teams play, there is often violence. Both teams continue to dominate the Scottish Premier League, and their rivalry is one of the longest-running and most well known. Small though it is, Scotland has produced some of Britain's most memorable soccer players: Dennis Law, Kenny Dalglish, Billy Bremner, and Graham Souness. The country has also produced some of Britain's best soccer managers, including Jock Stein; Sir Matt Busby, who managed the 1996 English World Cup team; Bill Shankly; and Alex Ferguson, who was in charge of England's most successful soccer team of all time, Manchester United, for nearly thirty years.

Rugby is also popular. Scotland's national team competes in the annual Six Nations Championship and the Rugby World Cup, while its two professional clubs enjoy enthusiastic fan support. The Glasgow Warriors represent the west part of the country, and Edinburgh Rugby the east.

On March 16, 2019, rugby player Ben Toolis of Scotland wins the ball in a lineout during the Guinness Six Nations match between England and Scotland at Twickenham Stadium.

GOLF

Tradition claims that golf was invented on the sand dunes of the east coast of Scotland. An early form of golf was played by Mary, Queen of Scots, who was said to have played golf shortly after the murder of her second husband. Golf is more popular and less expensive and elitist in Scotland than in the rest of Britain. Scotland has more than four hundred golf courses, with more greens per square mile of territory than any other country in the world. Most people play on public golf courses, which are owned by local councils, but there are many private courses, which are more expensive and exclusive. In very remote areas of Scotland, there are no caretakers for the golf courses, and players using a course are asked to put the greens fee in an honesty box.

The Royal and Ancient Golf Club, the worldwide governing body of the game, is based in Saint Andrews, Fife. Saint Andrews has six courses; the most famous is the Old Course, with only eleven instead of the standard eighteen greens and two short holes instead of four.

OTHER SPORTS

Besides being an occupation, fishing in Scotland is also a major leisure pursuit. Scotland has hundreds of miles of inland waterways and an enormous coastline, all perfect places for people keen on fishing. Fishing licenses are seldom necessary, and game fish such as trout and salmon are abundant.

Surfing is also popular in Scotland, which is unusual given its cold climate. Avid surfers head for the north coast, where at times the waves are comparable with those of Hawaiʻi. Skiing has been introduced only somewhat recently.

Surfers brave the waves on a cold winter's day at East Beach in Lossiemouth, Moray.

There are small ski resorts in the Cairngorms, Glencoe, Glenshee, and Nevis Range, where it is best to ski in February and sometimes March. In the same area, the Siberian Husky Club holds annual races.

Curling, another Scottish sport, was invented about five hundred years ago. It is similar to the English game of lawn bowling but is played on ice. Players slide curling stones across the ice at a target. The stones, which have a handle, are circular, slightly flat, and very heavy. Players are allowed to clear the loose snow in front of the stone as it moves. The player whose stone is nearest the target wins the game. Curling is an official Olympic sport.

Tennis is very much a part of Scottish history, and Scotland claims to have the oldest tennis court in the world, the Royal Tennis Court at Falkland. Scottish tennis players who have played in and won some of the greatest championships include Bobby Wilson and Winnie Shaw. In 2016, Scotsman Andy Murray was ranked numbet 1 in the world, but injuries have set him back in more recent years. He is a three-time Grand Slam tournament winner, a two-time Olympic champion, a Davis Cup champion, and a winner of the 2016 ATP World Tour Finals. Sir Andrew was knighted in 2017.

The Lawn Tennis Association (LTA) and Tennis Scotland have been working hard to make the game more accessible to everyone in Scotland.

INTERNET LINKS

https://www.scottishfa.co.uk
This is the site of the Scottish Football Association.

https://www.scottishrugby.org
More information about Scottish rugby can be found here.

http://www.shga.co.uk
The Scottish Highland Games Association has information and photos pertaining to the games.

FESTIVALS

A street performer entertains the public in August 2019 at the start of Edinburgh's Festival Fringe season.

12

B EING A PART OF THE UNITED Kingdom, Scotland observes most of the same special days as England, Wales, and Northern Island. Those holidays include the major Christian holidays of Christmas, Good Friday, and Easter, and a group of "bank holidays." Those are official days off when most people have the day off from school or work—and, appropriately, the banks are closed.

In addition to those, there's a long list of local festivals, many of which are based on ancient customs. Other festive occasions celebrate music and the arts, sports, whisky, food, literature, and more. The Royal Edinburgh Military Tattoo, for example, takes place in August and celebrates the country's military with great pomp and circumstance, with parades of military bands, pipers and drummers, and fireworks.

HOGMANAY

When it comes to fireworks, there is no greater occasion in Scotland than Hogmanay. This is the Scots' New Year's Eve celebration. It most likely gets its name from an old French, Gaelic, or Norse term—no one knows the origin for certain, but it dates back centuries for sure. Hogmanay is one of the most important festivals in Scotland, having upstaged Christmas in significance as long ago as the Reformation. It possibly has

Candlemas, on February 2, marks the day the baby Jesus was first presented at the temple. It marks the turning point of the year, when the worst of winter is over, and corresponds to the feast day of Saint Bridget in the Gaelic calendar. In Scotland, there is an old saying: "If Candlemas Day be bright and fair, half the winter is to come and mair (more). If Candlemas Day be dark and foul, half the winter was over at Yowl (Christmas)."

its roots in ancient solstice celebrations. Until modern times, gifts were given to children at Hogmanay rather than at Christmas.

An event that takes place in the early hours of New Year's morning is called "first footing." Great importance is placed on the nature of the first person to step over the threshold in the new year. The first choice is a tall, handsome, dark-haired stranger, although in some areas blond or red-haired visitors are best. Women may not be first footers, because they are deemed to bring bad luck. The first footer must bring gifts— fuel for the fire, bread or salt so that the family will not go hungry, and whisky. In another tradition practiced for the good luck of the house, the back door is opened just before midnight to let out the old year. As the new year begins, the front door is opened to let it in.

In some regions of Scotland, an even more ancient tradition is played out on Hogmanay—burning out the old year. In Comrie, there is a torchlight procession led by costumed people who light torches attached to 6-foot (1.8 m) poles. They parade around the village to the tunes of pipers and then throw the torches down in the middle of the square. Everyone dances around the fire until the embers burn out. In Wick, a huge bonfire, built over the previous two months, is lit in a park. In Biggar, the bonfire is built big enough to last all night, while revelers toast kippers in the flames.

FIRE FESTIVALS

There are more fire-centered ceremonies too. In the early hours of January 1 at Stonehaven, residents go through the town whirling fireballs around their heads to drive away evil spirits and welcome the New Year. In Burghead, on January 11, which was the end of the year before the calendars changed in 1752, a metal basket called a *clavie* (CLA-vy) is filled with tar-soaked wood. The clavie used to be specially molded for the occasion, but these days, a tar barrel or a whisky cask is used. At 6:00 p.m., it is lit with a piece of peat from a household fire, and men take turns carrying this burning barrel on their heads through the town. They must not trip, or mischief will befall the whole village the following year. As they go around the village, the men give smoldering pieces of wood to everyone they pass to bring them luck. Eventually, the clavie ends up on an ancient mound, where it is smashed to pieces, and revelers fight for pieces of lucky wood.

In January, the Shetland Islands have fire festivals. The biggest fire festival—at Lerwick on the last Tuesday in January—is known as Up Helly Aa. This marks the end of the old festival of Yule, which is still celebrated in Shetland. In the past, barrels of burning tar were dragged through the village on sleds by *guisards*, or men in strange costumes. A very rowdy event, it was consequently suppressed. The festival was altered somewhat when it was revived in the nineteenth century.

Since 1889, a 30-foot (9 m) Viking longship has been built each year. When the parade begins, the man elected as the *guizer jarl*, or master of ceremonies, stands on the ship with a band of men dressed as Vikings. The ship is pulled

In Gulberwick on the Shetland Islands, a celebration of Up Helly Aa lights the night.

through the town followed by the pipers and other guisards in their wild costumes. At a designated location, the Vikings jump off the ship, which is then burned. The guisards spend the rest of the night reveling.

WHUPPITY SCOORIE

The name of this festival is taken from a creature in a Scottish fairy tale, a story similar to that of Rumpelstiltskin. The creature was a bad fairy who could be defeated only by someone who guessed her name.

In Lanark, church bells are not rung during the months from October to February. Whuppity Scoorie on March 1 marks the beginning of spring, when the bells are rung for the first time of the year. At the first stroke of the bells, local children parade clockwise around the church, whirling paper balls around their heads. When the bells have finished ringing, the children compete to be the first to run three times around the church. Then, the provost of the church throws a handful of coins, and the children move hurriedly to catch them.

Traditionally, the ceremony was carried out by men, and they waved their hats over their heads. This hat waving often became rowdy and turned into fights, so the Victorians banned it. The essential ingredients of the festival— running clockwise round the church and whirling objects—probably dates back to a pagan ceremony to ward off evil spirits.

JEDBURGH BALL GAME

Jedburgh is one of the last remaining towns in Scotland to continue the tradition of a ball game on Candlemas, which falls on February 2. According to one tradition, the game was originally played with the severed heads of Englishmen. In modern times, the balls are made of leather and stuffed with straw. Two teams of Uppies and Doonies—those who live north of the market square and those who live south—play out a vicious game of handball. The Uppies have to get the ball to their side of town, and the Doonies to theirs. At some stage, the game ends on the frozen Jed River, and men commonly end up in the icy water.

The most famous of Scotland's modern festivals is the arts festival that takes place in Edinburgh in late summer. The Edinburgh International Festival claims to be the largest festival in the world. It first took place in 1947 and was intended to be— and still is—a very highbrow affair, with lots of performances of classical music and opera. However, that first year, eight theater groups turned up uninvited and performed in church halls around the city. It was this

unorganized element of the festival that gave rise to the Edinburgh Festival Fringe, which is one of the main attractions for people at the festival today.

The two events take place in mid to late August, and since 2015, they have been planned to coincide. Over the years, hundreds of famous people have performed there; in some cases, their Edinburgh show was what made them famous. Events range from operas to stand-up comedy, circus shows to street theater. A jazz festival has been added, as well as a television and film festival, and the Edinburgh Military Tattoo also takes place during the festival.

About one-third of the tickets are bought by local people; the rest are purchased by visitors from around the world. Hotels and other accommodations fill up—every hall, school, and pub is used. On Festival Sunday, a huge parade takes place in Holyrood Park in Edinburgh, with fireworks and a concert in the evening.

RIDING OF THE MARCHES

The Riding of the Marches is an ancient custom that was practiced in the border towns of Scotland during the Middle Ages. In some places, it is a tradition that commemorates a local historical incident, most likely conflicts between the Scottish and the English. The Riding, which involves gangs of young men galloping on horses around the town boundaries, is observed once a year during summer.

In Linlithgow, 16 miles (26 km) west of Edinburgh, the ceremony is particularly spectacular, with old-fashioned carriages and men dressed as heralds, halberdiers, and bailies—all ancient characters in the town's history. At Selkirk, a standard bearer is chosen, and he parades through the town with a pipe-and-drum band. This is called crying the burley—that is, calling all the riders to the ceremony. Banners of local regiments and craft guilds are taken out of storage and decorated with flowers before the parade begins. At the end of the Riding, the procession returns to town, and the flags are whirled around. In the afternoon, there is a horse race.

GAELIC SAMHAIN

Samhain (SOW-in), or Samhuinn, is a two-day Celtic fire festival held on October 31 and November 1, marking the end of summer and the beginning of winter. It was the most significant holiday of the Celtic year, as this was when the Celts celebrated the New Year. The Celts believed that at the time of Samhain, the ghosts of the dead were able to mingle with the living. People gathered to sacrifice livestock, fruits, and vegetables, and to light giant bonfires to honor the dead. The Celts believed that these acts helped the spirits carry on with their journey and kept them separated from the living. Costumes and masks were also worn to copy the spirits or placate them, and young men dressed in white wore masks or veils to impersonate the ghosts.

The festival became associated with the Christian All Saints' Day and All Souls' Day. It has also largely influenced the secular customs now connected with Halloween, which is celebrated on October 31. Although many customary elements of Halloween feature in Samhain celebrations, there is more focus on the rebirth of the year and the honoring of the dead during Samhain.

OTHER FESTIVALS

Scotland has many other festivals. A number of them are held in summer, aimed partly at the thousands of tourists who come to visit. In October, there is the Royal National Mod, where Gaelic events, including Gaelic song and poetry competitions, piping competitions, and other performances, are held. In September, a prominent event in the Highland Games is held at Braemar, and the Ben Nevis Race is run, in which amateurs race to the top of Scotland's highest mountain. June sees the hockey finals at Inverness and the Royal Highland Agricultural Show in Edinburgh. In May, there is another arts festival, this time in Glasgow, where a folk-music festival is also held in July.

Saint Andrew's Day (November 30) is a festival celebrated by expatriate Scots more than those who live in Scotland. Expatriate communities celebrate with pipe bands; ceilidhs, or parties; traditional food such as sheep's head and haggis; and whisky. In Scotland, it is celebrated with a religious service in Saint Andrews, where the saint's bones are kept.

INTERNET LINKS

https://www.theedinburghreporter.co.uk/2019/09/edinburgh-riding-of-the-marches-2019
Photos and a brief article capture the pomp of the annual Riding of the Marches in Edinburgh.

https://www.edintattoo.co.uk
The official site of the Royal Edinburgh Military Tattoo presents a history and photos.

https://www.scotlandinfo.eu/calendar-of-annual-events-and -festivals-in-scotland
This site presents a month-by-month listing of Scottish festivals.

https://www.timeanddate.com/holidays/uk
This calendar site lists the holidays and observances for the United Kingdom.

FOOD

The Foodie Festival in Edinburgh attracts hungry people from far and wide.

13

EVER SINCE THE LEGENDARY ROBERT Burns penned his laudatory ode to a lowly peasant dish in 1787, that unattractive food item has been the national dish of Scotland. Many people would probably agree that the brownish-gray bag of offal looks rather awful. Some say it tastes the same, though others report a "delicious savory flavor." Haggis, as it's called, is the butt of many jokes; nevertheless, it is the adored star of Scottish cookery—a cuisine characterized by humble foods with whimsical names.

Scottish cuisine was for many centuries centered on making use of every last scrap of food available. Lots of traditional dishes around the world are based on this frugal attitude. In modern times, Scots have developed a sweet tooth, and there are many desserts and cakes that are found only in Scotland. Immigrant communities have recently formed in the cities, and Indian and Chinese restaurants are the result of this cultural melting pot. In the 1980s and 1990s, increased wealth meant that people had more time for leisure activities and no longer regarded food as merely a matter of survival. In the cities, restaurants serving cuisines from other parts of Europe and beyond have opened.

"Address to a Haggis"
by Robert Burns
(excerpt)

Fair fa' your honest,
sonsie face /
Great chieftain o the
puddin'-race! /
Aboon them a' ye tak
your place, /
Painch, tripe, or
thairm: /
Weel are ye worthy
o' a grace /
As lang's my arm.

(translation)
Good luck to you and
your honest, plump
face / Great chieftain
of the sausage
race! / Above them
all you take your
place, / Stomach,
tripe, or intestines: /
Well are you worthy
of a grace / As long
as my arm.

HAGGIS

Haggis is a sheep's stomach filled with chopped organ meat, oatmeal, onions, and spices, simmered in a pot of water until cooked. It is traditionally served with "bashed neeps" (mashed turnip) and "chappit tatties" (mashed potatoes) and is especially popular on Burns Night, the anniversary of Robert Burns's birthday. Burns once wrote a poem dedicated to haggis, calling it "the great chieftain o' the puddin' race." (In this usage, "pudding" means sausage.) There is even a vegetarian version of haggis.

Every year, a competition is held for the tastiest haggis, and butchers all over Scotland compete for the honor. Haggis is readily available in Scottish chippies, or local fast-food outlets, where it is served in a small sausage shape and deep-fried. Until the twentieth century, haggis was as common in the rest of Britain as it is now in Scotland. It was only increasing wealth that drove the humble dish off English menus.

A knife cuts open a large haggis as part of a **Burns Night** celebration in **Edinburgh**.

BREAKFAST

There are several types of Scottish breakfast foods to choose from. Least healthy but very popular with the Scots (and tourists) is the full Scottish breakfast, which consists of fried eggs, bacon, sausage, tomatoes, and white or black pudding, which is a kind of blood sausage. Another Scottish breakfast dish is Arbroath smokies, known in England as kippers. Invented in Finnan, a village near Aberdeen, the dish consists of lightly smoked herring served with butter. Another alternative is smoked haddock served with a poached egg on top.

Butteries, also known as Aberdeen rolls or "rowies," are sometimes served as a second course after the hot dish. They are a bread- or pastry-like specialty of the Aberdeen area, although they are sold all over Scotland. Unlike croissants, they are round and brown, but like croissants, they have a high butter content, which makes them very soft. They are served warm with butter.

A traditional full Scottish breakfast can be seen here.

A hearty bowl of Scotch broth is served up in a farmhouse kitchen.

Another breakfast choice in Scotland is oatcakes. Called "breed" in northeast Scotland, these are made with oatmeal and bacon fat. The ingredients are mixed into a dough with warm water and then cut into rounds, which are quickly fried on a griddle and then left to dry out.

Scottish oatmeal or porridge comes in many forms, including instant microwavable packets. Traditional porridge is made with pinhead oats, or oats that have not been crushed or rolled. The porridge takes about forty-five minutes to cook and is served with salt and a side dish of cold milk. The oatmeal is spooned up and then dipped in the milk, and the little island of oatmeal sitting in the spoonful of milk is eaten. Scots never mix their oatmeal and milk together in one bowl.

TRADITIONAL MAIN COURSES

Like the rest of Western Europe, the Scots have access to all the luxuries of the supermarket, including instant meals and imported sauces and breads. A traditional Scottish evening meal might consist of Scotch broth, mince and tatties, cullen skink, stovies, and clapshot.

Scotch broth is a thick, wholesome soup made of various ingredients. The most important is barley, cooked with a mixture of either lamb or beef and vegetables. The combined ingredients are cooked for two hours or more. In the old days, the Scotch broth pot never left the stove; the last batch of broth formed the stock for a new pot of broth with a new set of ingredients. Cock-a-leekie is a soup of chicken and leeks with barley or rice.

"Mince and tatties" is similar to the English shepherd's pie. Ground beef, onions, and pinhead oatmeal are fried and then mixed with some vegetables and braised in gravy. The dish is then served with boiled potatoes. "Cullen skink" is a soup made from smoked haddock, onions, and potatoes that originated in

Cullen, a small town on the Moray Firth. It forms a thick, meaty stew rather than a thin soup and can be served with bread.

"Stovies" are a good way to use leftover cooked meat. Potatoes and onions are cooked with gravy until tender, and then the cooked meat is added along with seasonings. This is a very old dish with roots in the lives of the working poor, but it is often served at traditional ceilidhs and even weddings. It is usually served with oatcakes and a glass of milk. "Clapshot" is not a main dish but an accompaniment to meat dishes. It is a mixture of mashed potatoes, turnips, and onions.

SCOTTISH PUDDINGS

Scots prefer puddings—baked or boiled desserts—often the sweeter and stickier the better. As a rule, most cakes in Britain are also found in Scotland but with the addition of a layer of confectioners' sugar or granulated sugar. Scottish puddings include clootie dumpling, cranachan, and Scots pancakes. A particularly sweet dessert dish is Atholl brose.

A Christmas fruit pudding is a taste of traditional cuisine throughout the United Kingdom.

Clootie dumpling is a mixture of fruitcake ingredients combined with lots of spices, molasses, and suet, all wrapped in a cloth and simmered in water for about four hours. This is served with custard or brandy butter and is similar in taste to the Christmas pudding served in Britain on Christmas Day. Any leftovers can be fried and served again.

Cranachan is the traditional harvest dish and is a very luxurious dessert. It is sometimes served at weddings. The table is laid with oatmeal, cream, heather honey, whisky, and raspberries. The family sits down and serves themselves with whatever combination of these ingredients they love. Scots pancakes are made as a rich, creamy batter and then dropped a spoonful at a time on a hot griddle and cooked on both sides. They are served with Dundee preserves, a type of marmalade.

The traditional New Year dessert is called black bun and is a fruitcake baked within pastry. Other Scottish sweet things are shortbreads made with lots of butter.

Thick marmalade adorns pancakes in this sweet Scottish treat.

EATING OUT

The Scots have a good choice of places to eat, from authentic Indian and Chinese restaurants to Italian trattorias, pizza places, and brasserie-style cafés where a mix of traditional Scottish and innovative California-style dishes predominate.

Fine dining is available in the larger cities. At the other end of the market, the "chippies" are still going strong, as fish and chips (fried fish and french fries) are a popular choice among Scots. Fast-food outlets fill the main shopping areas, and trendy café bars offer wine, coffee, and light meals.

DRINKS

The most popular soft drink in Scotland is a fruit-flavored drink called Irn-Bru. Tea is the next most commonly consumed beverage. It is served very hot and strong, with milk and sugar added. Beer is popular among adults.

The national drink of Scotland is, of course, whisky, a name borrowed from the Gaelic *uisge-beatha*, "the water of life." Scottish records note that the earliest description of whisky making dates from 1494. Whisky grew in popularity after 1780, when a tax on wine made wine unaffordable for most people. It was estimated that there were eight licensed and four hundred illegal stills in operation then. The government clamped down on illegal whisky distilling, driving many of the stills underground. In 1823, the production of whisky was legalized.

A whisky distillery gleams in Speyside.

INTERNET LINKS

http://www.robertburns.org.uk/Assets/Poems_Songs/toahaggis.htm
Robert Burns's poem "Address to a Haggis" can be found on this page, along with a modern translation.

https://www.scotland.org/about-scotland/food-and-drink/scottish-recipes
Traditional and updated Scottish recipes are found on this site.

https://theculturetrip.com/europe/united-kingdom/scotland/articles/16-foods-you-must-eat-in-scotland
Photos and descriptions of Scotland's most iconic foods are posted on this site.

RUMBLEDETHUMPS

Also spelled "rumpledethumps," this casserole of potatoes and cabbage makes use of leftovers. Turnips, kale, and cheese are often added. Amounts are approximate and need not be precise.

1 ½ pounds mashed potatoes,
   or leftovers
1 pound rutabaga turnip, peeled,
   boiled, and mashed, or leftovers
2 ounces butter
9 ounces Savoy cabbage and/or
   kale, finely sliced
salt and pepper to taste
½ cup cheddar cheese, grated

Preheat the oven to 350°F. Butter a baking dish.

Place the mashed potato and turnip into a large mixing bowl; set aside.

Melt half of the butter in a frying pan. Add the cabbage and/or kale, and cook over medium-low heat until softened but not brown.

Add the vegetable(s) to the potato mixture, add the remaining butter, and mash together thoroughly. Season with salt and pepper.

Place the mixture in a baking dish, sprinkle the cheese on top, cover with foil, and bake in the oven for about 30 minutes or until heated right through. Remove the foil, and cook for another 5 minutes or until golden brown and a little crispy on the top.

Serve hot.

OATY BISCUITS

In Scotland and England, "biscuit" is the word for "cookie."

2 cups Scottish rolled oats
1 ½ cups flour
4 ounces butter, melted
1 Tbsp or more of honey
½ cup sugar
1 tsp baking soda
1 Tbsp water
pinch of salt
powdered sugar

Line a baking sheet with parchment paper.

Mix flour, baking soda, sugar, and salt in a bowl. Add oats, melted butter, and honey. Mix well. If the mixture is a bit dry, add the water.

Hand roll the mixture into small balls. Place on a baking sheet, and press down on each ball with a fork.

Bake at 350°F for 10—15 minutes. Remove from oven and let cool on the pan for 5 minutes.

Remove biscuits from pan, and move them to a plate. When cool, sprinkle with powdered sugar.

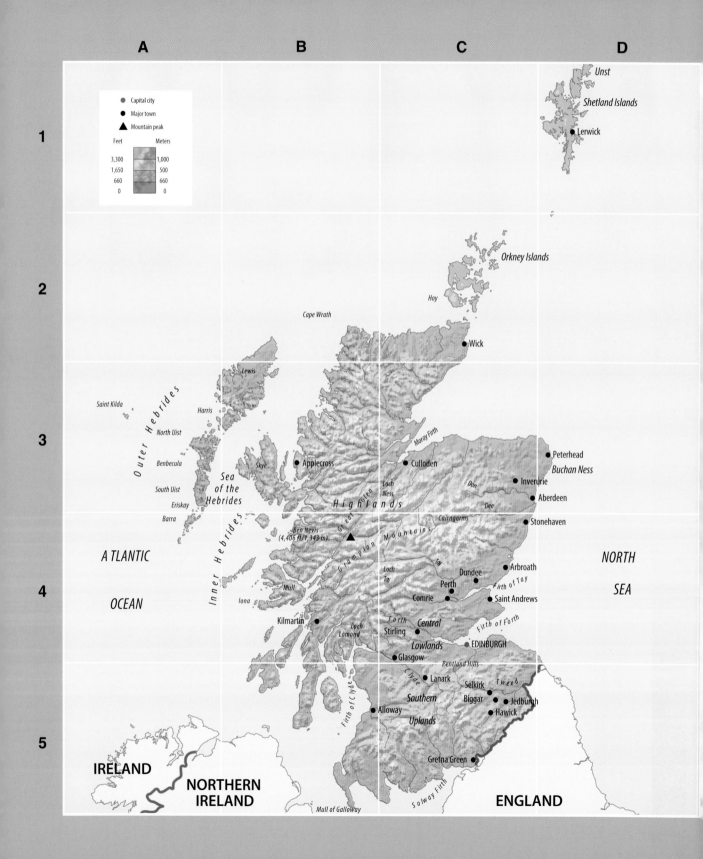

MAP OF SCOTLAND

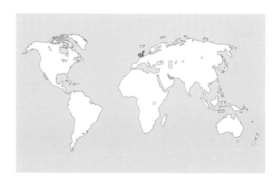

133

ECONOMIC SCOTLAND

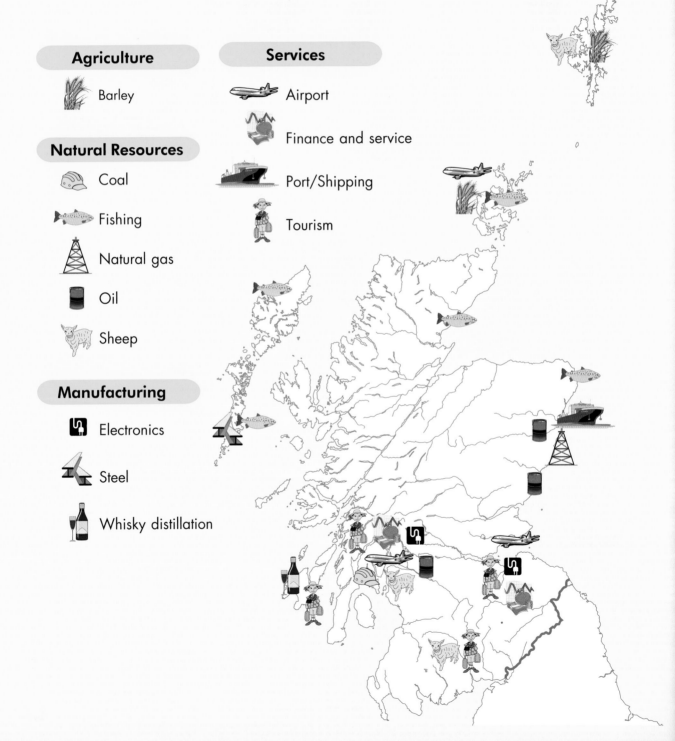

Agriculture

Barley

Natural Resources

Coal

Fishing

Natural gas

Oil

Sheep

Manufacturing

Electronics

Steel

Whisky distillation

Services

Airport

Finance and service

Port/Shipping

Tourism

ABOUT THE ECONOMY

All figures are 2017 estimates unless otherwise noted.

ABOUT THE ECONOMY
GDP $237,618,000

GDP per capita
$43,740 (2018)

MAIN EXPORTS
food and drink; professional, scientific, and technical services; petroleum and chemicals; mining and quarrying materials

MAIN EXPORT DESTINATIONS
United States, Netherlands, France, Germany, China, Ireland

MAIN IMPORTS
fuels—gas, natural and manufactured; office and automatic data processing machinery; power-generating machinery; machinery and transport equipment; apparel; clothing accessories

MAIN IMPORT PARTNERS
Norway, United States, China, Germany, Netherlands

CURRENCY
Pound sterling (GBP, symbolized £)
$1 = £0.81 (September 2019)

INFLATION RATE
2.48 percent (2018)

UNEMPLOYMENT RATE
3.9 percent (2018)

CULTURAL SCOTLAND

Aberdeen Maritime Museum
This award-winning museum is located near the heart of Aberdeen. It showcases displays on shipbuilding, fast sailing ships, fishing, and port history. It is also the only place in the UK to show displays on the North Sea oil and gas industry. The Provost Ross House, the second-oldest house in Aberdeen, built in 1593, is also part of the museum.

Duthie Park
Duthie Park consists of 44 acres (18 ha) of sprawling gardens donated by Lady Elizabeth Duthie in 1881. It is also home to greenhouses that make the park a popular place with visitors even during the cold winter months.

Meigle Sculptured Stone Museum
The museum features a collection of twenty-seven carved Pictish stones from the ninth century CE. The stones, believed to be monuments to dead Pictish warriors, were found mostly in the village of Meigle. These stones are housed permanently in an old schoolhouse that has been converted into a museum.

Camperdown Wildlife Center
This wildlife center is located within the premises of the Camperdown Country Park. Many of the animals that can be found here are endangered or threatened in the wild, such as the lynx and the snowy owl. The wildlife center also hosts many events that are both fun and educational.

Loch Ness and Inverness
Inverness is the capital city of the Scottish Highlands, and a short distance away from it is the famed Loch Ness, where many visitors go in the hopes of sighting the mythical Loch Ness Monster.

Glamis Castle
Situated about 12 miles (19 km) from the city of Dundee, Glamis is known for its beautiful architecture and history. The castle was the childhood home of the late Queen Mother and the ancestral home of the Earls of Strathmore, and it is part of the inspiration for one of Shakespeare's most renowned plays, *Macbeth*. It has more than six hundred years of history behind it and is reputed to be one of the most haunted castles in Scotland.

Glasgow Cathedral
Glasgow Cathedral has been in use for more than eight hundred years and is a good example of Scottish Gothic architecture. The cathedral is said to be built over the site where Saint Mungo, the patron saint of Glasgow, had built his church. The cathedral was built before the Reformation.

HMS *Unicorn*
The HMS *Unicorn* was a fast and powerful warship with forty-six cannons that was launched in 1824. It gets its name from its white unicorn figurehead and is one of the six oldest ships in the world. Visitors get to learn about the history of the ship, as well as experience what a warship was like in the days of yore.

The David Livingstone Center
The center is housed in the tenement block where David Livingstone once lived, which was converted into a museum in 1929. Here, the world-famous Scottish explorer's personal belongings and the equipment he used on expeditions are on display.

Edinburgh Castle
Built on an extinct volcano, the castle dates as far back as the twelfth century and was one of the country's most important fortresses. Visitors are able to view Scottish royal regalia, a World War II memorial, and cannons that once defended the land.

Children's International Theater Festival
Every year, over the period of a week, in different venues across Edinburgh, children are offered the opportunity to watch a variety of award-winning theatrical productions from all over the world.

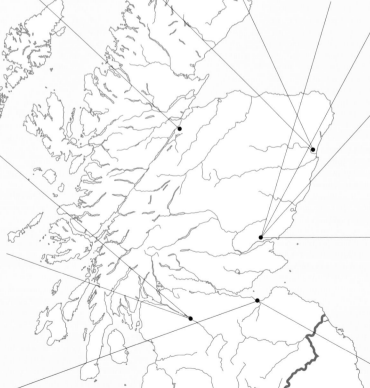

ABOUT THE CULTURE

OFFICIAL NAME
Scotland

CAPITAL
Edinburgh

FLAG
Saint Andrew's Cross, or Saltire

ANTHEM
Official UK anthem: "God Save the Queen"
Unofficial Scottish anthems: "Flower of
Scotland" and "Scotland the Brave"

GOVERNMENT
constitutional monarchy

MAJOR CITIES
Glasgow, Edinburgh, Aberdeen, Dundee

POPULATION
5,440,000 (2019 estimate)

POPULATION GROWTH
0.2 percent (2018)

ETHNIC GROUPS
white 94 percent; Asian 3 percent (includes
Pakistani, 1 percent); black, African, or
Caribbean 1 percent; mixed race
0.4 percent; other 0.3 percent (2011)

LANGUAGES
English, Scottish Gaelic, Scots

RELIGIONS
Christianity 32 percent (includes Church
of Scotland); Muslim 1.4 percent; Buddhist,
Hindu, Sikh 0.7 percent; no religion
37 percent; Jewish 0.001 percent (2011)

LIFE EXPECTANCY AT BIRTH
Male: 77.1 years
Female: 81.2 years (2015)

INFANT MORTALITY RATE
3.7 deaths per 1,000 live births (2018)

LITERACY
99 percent

TIMELINE

IN SCOTLAND	IN THE WORLD
574–608 CE Scottish kingdom of Dál Riata reaches its peak of power under king Áedán mac Gabráin.	
	600 CE Height of the Mayan civilization is reached.
889–900 The reign of Domhnall mac Custantín, the first king described with the title Rí Alban, signifies the absorption of Picts by Gaelic kings and an emergent Scottish identity.	**1000** The Chinese perfect gunpowder and begin to use it in warfare.
1295 Signing of the Auld Alliance between Scotland and France takes place.	
1296 Annexation of Scotland by England occurs.	
1320 The pope accepts the Declaration of Arbroath that recognizes Scottish independence from England.	**1530** Beginning of transatlantic slave trade is organized by the Portuguese in Africa.
1642 Civil war breaks out in England.	
1707 The Acts of Union are passed, and Scotland is formally united with England to form Great Britain.	**1776** US Declaration of Independence is written.
	1789–1799 The French Revolution takes place.
	1914 World War I begins.
	1939 World War II begins.
1943 More than one thousand people are killed over two days in Clydebank and southern Glasgow during the only sustained German bombing attack on Scotland during World War II.	**1945** The United States drops atomic bombs on Japan. World War II ends.
	1969 US astronaut Neil Armstrong becomes the first human on the moon.
	1986 Nuclear power disaster occurs at Chernobyl in Ukraine.
	1991 Breakup of the Soviet Union takes place.

IN SCOTLAND	IN THE WORLD
1997	**1997**
Voters approve a referendum for a separate Scottish Parliament after 290 years of union with England. The Scotland Act is passed in favor of devolution of powers to Scotland.	Britain returns Hong Kong to China.
1999	
Scotland holds its first national election in 300 years, and a Scottish Parliament is reinstated.	**2001**
	Al-Qaeda terrorists stage 9/11 attacks in New York, Washington, DC, and Pennsylvania.
2003	**2003**
Scotland holds its second election. Labour wins 50 seats, followed by the SNP with 27 seats.	War in Iraq begins.
2004	
Royal opening of Scottish Parliament at Holyrood occurs.	
2007	
The third general election is held. The SNP wins the largest representation with 47 seats.	**2008**
	US elects first African American president, Barack Obama.
2009	**2009**
The Church of Scotland votes to allow gay men and women to become ministers.	Outbreak of H1N1 flu spreads around the world.
2014	
Scotland's referendum on national independence rejects independence. Alex Salmond resigns as first minister; Nicola Sturgeon, also of the SNP, becomes the first minister of the Scottish Parliament.	**2015–2016**
	ISIS launches terror attacks in Belgium and France.
2016	
UK-wide referendum on leaving the European Union (EU), dubbed Brexit, passes, though Scotland votes overwhelmingly to remain in the EU.	**2017**
	Donald Trump becomes US president. Hurricanes devastate Houston, Caribbean islands, and Puerto Rico.
	2018
	Winter Olympics are held in South Korea.
2019	**2019**
Matters regarding Brexit spur discussion of possible new referendum on Scottish independence.	Terrorist attacks mosques in New Zealand. Notre Dame Cathedral in Paris damaged by fire. Hurricane Dorian ravages the Bahamas.

GLOSSARY

Brexit
The process of the United Kingdom leaving the European Union.

ceilidh
A social gathering involving dancing, singing, storytelling, and drinking.

croft
A small area of land that usually combines a house and land for cultivating or grazing.

firth
An indentation of the seacoast; the mouth of a river.

Gaelic
The indigenous language of Scotland, one of several ancient Celtic languages.

guisards
Party-goers dressed in elaborate costumes at festival time.

haggis
A meal made of the chopped liver, heart, and lungs of sheep, seasoned with spices, stuffed into a sheep's stomach, and boiled.

Hogmanay
New Year's Eve.

Holyrood
A term for the Scottish government, taken from the section of Edinburgh where the Scottish Parliament meets.

kelpie
A mythical shape-shifting water spirit in Scottish legend.

Kirk
The Church of Scotland; or generically, a Scottish church.

pibroch
The classical music of the great Highland bagpipe.

pudding
A sausage; or a dessert.

shinty
A traditional Scottish game similar to modern hockey.

taigh tughaidh (TIE too-ee)
Literally "house of thatch," referring to the older type of croft houses.

Up Helly Aa
A fire festival held at Lerwick in the Shetland Islands that originated from an ancient Viking tradition.

FOR FURTHER INFORMATION

BOOKS

DK Travel. *DK Eyewitness Travel Guide Scotland*. New York, NY: DK Publishing, 2019.

Green, Jonathan. *Scottish Miscellany: Everything You Always Wanted to Know About Scotland the Brave*. New York, NY: Skyhorse Publishing, 2014.

Herman, Arthur. *How the Scots Invented the Modern World: The True Story of How Western Europe's Poorest Nation Created Our World & Everything in It*. New York, NY: Three Rivers Press, Random House, 2002.

National Archives of Scotland. *Tracing Your Scottish Ancestors: The Official Guide*. Edinburgh, UK: Birlinn, 2011.

Wilson, Neil, Andy Symington, and Sophie McGrath. *Lonely Planet Scotland*. Melbourne, Australia: Lonely Planet, 2019.

ONLINE

BBC News. Scotland. https://www.bbc.com/news/scotland

Creative Scotland. https://www.creativescotland.com

Encyclopædia Britannica. "Scotland." https://www.britannica.com/place/Scotland

The *Guardian*. Scotland. https://www.theguardian.com/uk/scotland

Historic Environment Scotland. https://www.historicenvironment.scot

National Museums Scotland. https://www.nms.ac.uk

The Scottish Government. https://www.gov.scot

Scotland Is Now. https://www.scotland.org/about-scotland

Visit Scotland. https://www.visitscotland.com

MUSIC

Hastings, Claire. *Those Who Roam*. Luckenbooth Records, 2019.

Fowlis, Julie. *Alterum,* Machair Records Ltd, 2017.

Franz Ferdinand. *You Could Have It So Much Better*. Rich Costey, 2005.

Newton, Abby. *Crossing to Scotland*. Culburnie Records, 1997.

Redpath, Jean. *The Songs of Robert Burns,* Greentrax, 2000.

Various artists. *Fiona Ritchie Presents: The Best of the Thistle & Shamrock*. Hearts of Space, 1999.

Various artists. *Traditional Music of Scotland*. Alliance, 2009.

Various artists. *Scotland: The Real Music from Contemporary Caledonia,* Smithsonian Folkways, 2003.

BIBLIOGRAPHY

BBC News. "Loch Ness Monster May Be a Giant Eel, Say Scientists." September 5, 2019. https://www.bbc.com/news/uk-scotland-highlands-islands-49495145.

BBC News. "Majority of Scots Say They Are 'Not Religious.'" September 17, 2017. https://www.bbc.com/news/uk-scotland-41294688.

CIA. *The World Factbook*. "United Kingdom." https://www.cia.gov/library/publications/the-world-factbook/geos/uk.html.

Encyclopædia Britannica. "Scotland." https://www.britannica.com/place/Scotland.

Keane, Kevin. "How to Tackle Scotland's 'Climate Emergency.'" BBC News, August 12, 2019. https://www.bbc.com/news/uk-scotland-49207097.

Kennouche, Sofiane. "Manufacturing in Scotland: What Do We Still Make?" *The Scotsman*, February 10, 2016. https://www.scotsman.com/news-2-15012/manufacturing-in-scotland-what-do-we-still-make-1-4026636.

Power Technology. "Scotland Renewable Energy Generation Reaches Record Levels." March 29, 2019. https://www.power-technology.com/news/scotland-renewable-energy-record.

Scotland's Census. "Ethnicity, Identity, Language, and Religion." https://www.scotlandscensus.gov.uk/ethnicity-identity-language-and-religion.

Scottish Government. https://www.gov.scot.

Stando, Olaf. "No-Deal Brexit Would Be Catastrophic for Our Daily Lives—Here's How." SNP, August 26, 2019. https://www.snp.org/how-a-no-deal-brexit-will-affect-our-daily-lives.

Visit Scotland. https://www.visitscotland.com.

INDEX

INDEX